WE WERE
WRONG

KEITH STEWART

WE WERE WRONG

AN EVANGELICAL PASTOR'S
RADICAL TRANSFORMATION THROUGH
FOLLOWING JESUS IN THE MARGINS

HISPUBLISHING
GROUP

www.hispubg.com

A division of HISpecialists, llc

HIS Publishing Group
1402 Corinth St., Suite 131
Dallas, TX 75225

HIS Publishing Group is a division of Human Improvement Specialists, llc.
For information visit www.hispubg.com or contact publisher
at info@hispubg.com

10 9 8 7 6 5 4 3 2 1

WE WERE WRONG
Summary: God changed a Pastor's heart in the slums of Africa
and the heart of a church in Dallas, Texas. —Provided by the publisher.

Library of Congress:
2014914830

ISBN-13:
978-0-9907152-0-7

1. Religion 2. Spiritual life 3. Inspirational

Dedication

*To Oliver
Thank you for simply being who you are!
Your life rescued mine.*

*100% of the profits from the sale of this book
will be given to global missions*

I was wrong. I'm sorry. These are among the most difficult words to say because they're so powerful. When my friend Keith Stewart put these words in a full-page ad in the local paper, they changed his life, his congregation, and impacted the lives of thousands and thousands of children around the world. Read this book and experience the power of those five little words.

—*Richard Stearns*, president World Vision US and author of *The Hole in Our Gospel* and *Unfinished*

Some pastors focus on winning converts for Jesus; others make the Kingdom ethics of Jesus their first love. Keith Stewart sees evangelism and social justice as two ways of describing the same mission. If you don't think American Christianity has a credibility problem you need to read this book. But Pastor Stewart's derives no joy from popping pious balloons. *We Were Wrong* leads the church through the awkward agony of repentance to an invigorating vision of authentic Christian discipleship.

—*Dr. Alan Bean*, executive director of Friends of Justice

My good friend, Keith Stewart, whose cutting edge church is making a significant impact in the greater Dallas area, and other parts of the world, has provided provocative insight on missional ministry. His personal journey of discovery to Kenya revolutionized the way he saw mission, and through this book, he provides a critical resource for others interested in global ministry. Having been in both city and international ministry for many years, I believe this is one of the most important new writings on the subject of missional theology and should be a must read for those on the same "journey of discovery."

—*Kathy H. Dudley*, D.Min., President of Imani Bridges

We all need to believe that change is possible. As Christians, we place our hope in a God who actually transforms minds and hearts. *We Were Wrong* tells the story of an amazing and spellbinding journey by a successful evangelical Pastor in Texas and his congregation into a full commitment to God's justice. At the same time, Rev. Keith Stewart communicates a vision of whole gospel discipleship that will make sense to people who may never have thought about comprehensive ministry with the poor or social justice as having any essential connection with their Christian faith. This is an important book; as a speaker and trainer in many evangelical circles, I plan to carry it around and hand it out!

—*Rev. Alexia Salvatierra*, co-author of *Faith-Rooted Organizing: Mobilizing the Church in Service to the World*

The idea that captivates me in this book is "Mutual Transformation." Mutual transformation starts as we connect our own poverty with the people we serve. God enjoys the company of those who want to be healed in this process. Mutual transformation is that which liberates us from the cynicism of humility without obedience or of the pursuit of success over transcendent purpose. Instead of imitating the successful ones, we can enjoy the journey of mutual transformation where God guides us. Pastor Keith writes with the prophetic authority of the broken heart that clings to the only Kingdom that is worthwhile and with the stubborn desire to encourage other churches to take their social action ministries on an adventure where God moulds the hearts of all those involved. Pray as you read this book and God will guide your heart to the place He desires to heal. We don't have any time to lose.

—*Jose Luis Ochoa*, Interim National Director for World Vision Ecuador

Few church communities have ever publicly admitted that they were wrong; fewer yet have worked as hard at turning things around than Keith Stewart and his church. Chronicling a journey from avoidance to encounter and conversion, this book draws us into the reign of God from the bottom up and leaves no doubt that more is yet to come.

—*Joerg Rieger*, Ph.D., Wendland-Cook Professor of Constructive
Theology, Perkins School of Theology, SMU

I believe Keith's book *We Were Wrong,* is one of the most important and urgently needed narratives of the Gospel of our time. As the Christian community dogmatically argues among themselves, a surrounding world in need of Jesus becomes more confused, concerned, and critical of the Christian faith. Keith's own story and enlightening revelations of the Gospel provide the clarity and understanding so desperately needed by so many. I know I did.

—*Bill Chiaravalle*, Principal of Brand Navigation and coauthor of
Branding for Dummies

My Father, Bob Pierce, always wanted to inspire others to step up to the plate and use their gifts to serve Christ without fear or apology. Pastor Keith Stewart has done just that with this book. Some people will find it hard to read. Others will find it hard to swallow. But I can guarantee that no one will read this book and shrug it off. My father was not afraid to make people feel uncomfortable...uncomfortable with the imbalance of suffering in the world ... uncomfortable with their own inertia ... uncomfortable with the status quo. Pastor Keith Stewart has that gift, too! People may not always appreciate you for making them uncomfortable, but when they get uncomfortable enough, they will move. And even the slightest movement towards compassion, generosity, and greater faith will change the world. Thank you for making us all a bit more uncomfortable!

—*Marilee Pierce Dunker*, daughter of Bob Pierce,
World Vision's Founder

One of the most important books to be written for the church in North America this century. *We Were Wrong* is written with a pastoral heart and a deep grounding in scripture. I was surprised over and over by biblical insights that were hiding in plain sight. I want to press this book into the hands of every pastor and Jesus-follower in the country.

—*Dr. Lydia Bean,* author of *The Politics of Evangelical Identity* (Princeton University Press, 2014)

TABLE OF CONTENTS

About the Author

Pastor Keith Stewart has been happily married to his wife Brenda for 30 years, has two daughters and one granddaughter with whom he is smitten.

Twenty-four years ago, Pastor Keith founded Springcreek in suburban Dallas, Texas. His church grew from a handful of people to 2500 who call Springcreek Church their home.

Pastor Keith is a tireless advocate for the world's poor. He has done extensive work with World Vision including; teaching missional theology for Pastor Vision Trips, consulting, conference speaking, fundraising and writing. He currently serves as a member of World Vision's Ministry Advisors Council.

In 2014, Pastor Keith was awarded the prestigious Bridge Builder Award by the Garland NAACP.

Springcreek Church has deep roots in the community that include; the largest disability ministry in the State of Texas, recovery ministries, elder care, ministry to prior offenders, homeless ministries and significant local church and civic partnerships.

FOREWORD

"Into the hovels of the poor,
Into the dark streets where the homeless groan,
God speaks: "I've had enough; I'm on my way
To heal the ache in the heart of the wretched."
PSALM 12.5 (THE MESSAGE)

"Let my heart be broken by the things that break the heart of God."
—BOB PIERCE, FOUNDER OF WORLD VISION

GOD HAS A PENCHANT FOR THE INAUSPICIOUS. What looks ordinary, hopeless, and mundane to us brims with possibility to God. In Scripture, God repeatedly seeks out the least and the last as His instrument of choice: Moses the stutterer, Gideon the chicken-hearted, Jonah the reluctant prophet, Peter the impetuous, and Mary the prostitute...you get the idea. But what disqualified them with men made them imminently usable with God.

This pattern shows up continually in God's Word, yet we seem to forget this essential truth in our daily lives. As a result, we end up looking for God where we are least likely to find Him: in the spectacular, the grandiose and most charismatic personalities. In our misdirection, we fail to hear God's still, small voice.

The still, small voice of God is still speaking today. Because it's still, we can't go rushing through life and expect to find it, and because it's small, we have to lean in and listen, or else we'll never hear it. Both of those characteristics suggest a God who prefers the inauspicious, the very people and circumstances we are most likely to dismiss.

X   (In practical terms, if this is God's preferred method of communication (unlikely people and inauspicious circumstances), then the people of God must intentionally seek Him where He is to be found.)

X   (When God has a message for His people, it is far more likely to show up wearing rags than a suit and tie.)It is far more likely to come through the voiceless and vulnerable than those who move in places of power and influence. We will find God in the slums more often than in suburbia, in the cry of the poor than in the shouts of the rich, and in conversations with those on the underside of power as opposed to those who hold all the power.

God is speaking, but we are tuned to the wrong frequency. There are literally thousands of still, small voices crying out to us today. Those voices are the Father's voice whose heart breaks that His Church has grown deaf.

Just such a conversation started my own journey six years ago. I could've easily ignored the voice myself, were it not for the fact that I was so desperate. Let me tell you what led to this encounter that literally changed my life.

I started my church 22 years ago. Springcreek Church was a seeker church that grew from a handful of people to a congregation of hundreds in a few short years. As a seeker church, we were fixated on the culture of cool and mass marketing of our "product." My preaching focused primarily on the needs of people. Staying abreast of the latest trends was more important to me than staying in sync with God's Spirit. I'm not saying that that's true of all seeker churches. No, I'm just trying to be honest about what was going on in me.

Over the years, the cumulative effect on me was quite negative. Don't get me wrong, the world didn't end. Our church was growing, people loved it, and we took pride in being the Rock n' Roll church. We had a reputation for pushing the edge of the envelope. As a result, we attracted a multitude of people who, for all intents and purposes, had been lost to the Church.

There's no question; good things were happening, and many decisions for Christ were made. We baptized new believers constantly. People told their friends, and my preaching seemed to be touching and changing lives. The result was years of growth and stability.

But long about year 15, I was finding it increasingly difficult to get out of bed. My motivation for pastoral ministry was at an all-time low. I had a nagging feeling that something wasn't right. Something wasn't right with me, with the church, and with the way we were doing ministry, but I couldn't tell you exactly what was missing.

I struggle with how best to describe what I was feeling. The analogy that comes to mind is a pyramid marketing scheme. Church for me had degenerated into endless recruitment of my down line. I was recruiting people to recruit more people so that they might recruit even more people to come to our services on the weekend. It was all about growing the weekend service. Whether we intended to be a recruiting organization or not, the practical reality was the majority of our budget, time, and energy was invested in having great weekend services. That's what fueled "the business." We wanted numbers, lots of numbers: attendance, offerings, decisions; everything and everyone were quantified. That's how we measured our "success."

Frankly, this left me feeling hollow, and I told God just that. "If this is what it means to be a successful pastor, I just don't want it anymore." Again, people weren't unhappy with me. Weekend services were still great. By all outward appearances, everything seemed fine, but I was dying inside and couldn't tell you why.

While wrestling with these feelings of dissonance, I attended a pastor's conference in San Diego. It was there I heard Tony Campolo speak. I can't tell you the title of his sermon that day, but there were two things that stood out to me about his message.

One unmistakable remembrance was that Campolo was full of passion. He preached like one who truly believed every word he was saying. Considering the fact I was feeling dead inside, it was quite refreshing to hear someone else speak from a place of deep conviction and belief. It made me wonder, "Could I ever feel that way again? Would anything about church ever move me that profoundly?"

X ⟨The other thing that stood out to me was his advocacy for the orphaned and vulnerable children of the world.⟩He believed in child sponsorship and thought every pastor in America should travel to Africa and see firsthand what was really transpiring there. That way, we would know why these kids were so very near and dear to God's heart.

I said to myself, "Maybe this is it. Maybe God wants me to help save Africa," not realizing at the time that what God really wanted was to bring Africa into my life to save me.

In October 2006, I contacted World Vision and made my first trip to Kenya. I had no idea at the time that a trip to a slum outside of Nairobi would hold for me the direction I'd been missing, the purpose to which I'd been called, and the satiation of the deepest hunger of my soul.

At first, the trip didn't hold much meaning at all. We were going into a slum called Soweto, a community that sprang up on the town garbage dump. In the developing world, these communities are fairly common, I was told. The dump is where the extra resources are. Many people, mired in deep poverty, exist off the throwaways of the rest of humanity. The stench was awful. The eyes I peered into seemed hollow and hopeless.

However, the need, as dire as it was, was not nearly as impactful as the love I saw in one orphan named Oliver. Oliver was a young man about 19 years old. Losing both parents at a young age had landed Oliver in World Vision's sponsor program. By the time he turned 18, it was apparent that this young man (and others like him) had no way to provide for himself. He had no marketable skill. To cut him loose from the sponsorship program would be to release him into the begging poverty of his community.

World Vision, sensing a gap in their developmental approach, started a program for young men like Oliver that would teach them business basics. Through teaching and mentorship, Oliver would learn the essentials of creating a business. Then, through microenterprise, World Vision would provide him the money to launch his business.

Oliver had done just that. Although he had not grown up in Soweto, he saw a business opportunity in this community built on top of Nairobi's garbage dump. He would sell mobile phone accessories. Oliver set up shop in a little 6'X 9' cinderblock building selling phone covers, lanyards, and rechargeable minutes for phones.

It always shocks Westerners when they travel to deeply impoverished corners of the world and find so many people using mobile phones, for we associate mobile phones with affluence. You have to understand that many of these countries that today rely heavily on mobile phones never had the capital to invest in the infrastructure for landlines to every home, so they skipped that entire technology and landed in the mobile phone era. Because postal delivery is often equally undeveloped, and many mobile users don't have credit for monthly plans anyway, mobile phones in the developing world are, for the most part, all pay as you go. For a few shillings, they can purchase a card that recharges their phones with minutes so they can make calls.

Oliver's big claim to fame, his "money-maker" (if you want to call it that), was a foot-long power strip that had cell phone chargers of every variety plugged into it. What Oliver had going for him that other residents of Soweto did not was electricity. The way Oliver made the bulk of his money was pennies at a time, charging the battery in the mobile phones of his clients.

Oliver was very proud of his tiny shop, as well he should have been. After showing me what he did to make his business work, Oliver revealed something to me I was not expecting. He introduced me to his business associate. Oliver had an apprentice, a young man like himself, orphaned by life's circumstances. Oliver was "teaching" him the business and sharing the profits with him.

The moment Oliver introduced me to his apprentice, I had the devastating realization of who was rich and who was poor. In this slum, surrounded by a kind of poverty I'd only heard about and never seen, there was a poverty in me that was even greater than that around me. It dawned on me as I stood in the dirt by this tiny shack that if I had grown up without a mom and dad, eked out an existence on the town garbage dump charging people's phones for a living, and was surrounded by this sea of desperate human need, I would have never dreamed of sharing what little I had with anybody else. Oliver was rich in ways in which I was desperately poor. This kid was rich in compassion, caring, generosity, and love; all I had was money.

In that moment I prayed, "Dear God, I can't go the rest of my life not having what this kid has."

God spoke in His still, small voice. A seemingly insignificant encounter in a Nairobi slum was the catalyst I needed to transform my life and church.

There was nothing charismatic about Oliver. He will likely never be remembered for his shack at the center of Soweto, but he is just the kind of person that God uses best. His life and his example got to me in ways that few others ever have.

God used Oliver as a mirror held up to my sick soul. When I looked at his life, it forced me to look at my own, and I didn't like what I saw. In short, his life was the wrench in the works. Oliver wrecked my life in all the ways it needed to be wrecked.

Oliver thought he was selling cell phone accessories, but he wasn't. He was selling hope. He was the instrument God used to show me my poverty, my desperate lack, my starving soul. Oliver helped me see that I was wasting my life in small purposes. I had bought into the lie that church was about growing numbers, the cult of celebrity, big buildings, impressive weekend services, and the endless catering to our own wants and desires. This way of doing ministry was killing me spiritually. God had taken me all the way to Africa to help me see my spiritual erosion.

It was a moment of radical clarity. Oliver was rich; I was poor, but I needed what he had. I had lost sight of what was most important, and what was missing in me was also missing in my church.

I knew what I had to do. Somehow, some way, I had to connect my church to this reality. The problem is, not everyone can make this trip, but of those that do, many will not make this connection. So how do I bridge an ocean and connect my safe suburban church with young people like Oliver who have so much to teach us?

For me, sponsorship was the answer. I simply had to bring sponsorship to my church, not just for the sake of kids like Oliver, but for our sake too. In our isolated, insulated suburban life, we had lost touch with reality. We had structured our lives in such a way as never to have to encounter extreme neediness in others, and because we had lost touch with it in them, we had lost touch with it within ourselves.

The Bible declares, *"and a little child shall lead them"* (Isaiah 11.6). That is so like God, isn't it? We are so enamored with the rich and the powerful, the movers and shakers. Like I said earlier, God's preferred method has always been *"the least of these"* (Matthew 25.40). God chooses the Olivers of the world to save the world. That has always been His way. We just abandoned His ways and went our own way.

Oliver thought he was a tiny businessman in a sprawling slum, but he wasn't. He was a seed planter and a hope giver. That day in Soweto, Oliver planted something in me that took root. A discouraged pastor, ready to walk away from the ministry, discovered in a Soweto slum that hope lives.

When Oliver stands before his Maker one day, I can hear the Father say, *"For I was hungry and you gave me something to eat, I was thirsty and you gave me something to drink, I was a stranger and you invited me in..."* (Matthew 25.35)

And Oliver, just like those first century disciples, will say, "But Lord, when did I see you hungry and feed you? When were you ever thirsty and I gave you something to drink? And Lord, for the life of me, I can never remember you even being in prison, let alone visiting you."

And Jesus will say, *"Whatever you did for one of the least of these... you did for me* (Matthew 25.40).

"Remember that pastor from Texas that came to visit you one day in Soweto? He was one of the least of these. You see, Oliver, he was starving for meaning and purpose, hungry for something to satisfy his soul. You gave it to him. Not just that, he was dying of thirst. He had tried to quench that thirst by building his own little kingdom, and you, Oliver, you led him back to the fountain of life. Although you couldn't see the prison bars that held him tight, he was imprisoned in an extremely self-serving lifestyle. You broke the lock and set him free. Oliver, you thought you were just selling mobile phone accessories, but you were changing the world."

The day I met Oliver was the day I finally understood what I'd been missing. This encounter was God's gift to me. I had lost my way, and God was giving me another chance. Little did I understand that what began on that day would change me forever.

Chapter 1

OUR APOLOGY
TO THE COMMUNITY

I N THE SUMMER OF 2008, I was out for a run at White Rock Lake in Dallas. Running for me is "God" time. It's time I use for extended prayer and meditation, for it takes me a good hour and a half to run the lake. With the beauty of the lake, the gentle sounds of the water, and the quietness of the trail, I just bring myself present to God. Sometimes I talk to God. Most times, I just listen. (My lake runs are sacred, dedicated time just to be with my Father. Whether or not anything is said or received, it's always good to be with Him.)

But on that day, as I was listening, I heard Him say, as distinctively as I've ever heard Him say anything, "I want you to apologize to the community for the kind of church you've been."

I knew exactly what He meant.

Following a seeker model for ministry all these years had made my church very good at producing consumers and horrible at producing disciples. Before Africa, our central mission could best be described as serving ourselves. Our "brand" of Christianity had had little to do with building the Kingdom of God. It was just another expression of baby-boomer me-ism. That's just the truth. It also happens to be the biggest regret I have in my ministry.

Please understand, my church is full of very good people. I love them all dearly. In speaking in generalities, I run the risk of making everyone feel indicted when I am sure there were many who were not pleased with the direction of the church. To those I offer my sincere apology. I did not serve you well during those years. More than anything, I want you to hear my ownership over my leadership failures. To the degree that affected the church, I want to be equally honest.

That day around White Rock Lake, I sensed God was giving me a path back, a way to restore lost credibility. He was showing me how to release the burden of regret that was weighing me down. It would take an acknowledgment, an apology to the community, confessing that we had lost our way, and in the process, failed them. So that's what we did. We took out a full-page ad in *The Dallas Morning News* that said…

WE WERE WRONG

"We followed trends when we should have followed Jesus.
We told others how to live but did not listen ourselves.
We live in a land of plenty, denying ourselves nothing,
While ignoring our neighbors who actually have nothing.
We sat on the sidelines while AIDS ravaged Africa.
We were wrong; we're sorry. Please forgive us."

That was all it said besides our church name, phone number, and website.

We did not explain because, as I've heard so many times, explanations at the point of apology sound like excuses. We needed to speak the truth about our behavior and offer a sincere apology to those we had wronged.

The apology was no gimmick. We had nothing to gain from it but the disdain of the Christian community and the hope of restored credibility in the eyes of the unbelieving community.

Needless to say, we were inundated by telephone calls. The vast majority of the calls were positive. An advertising executive called to say that though he'd been in the advertising business for more than 25 years, he had never seen a better use of ad space in his life. Others called to say they were moved to tears and grateful to hear an apology from the Church. Still others called to offer their encouragement, support, and prayers. There were even callers who thanked us for our courage.

There were also some, definitely in the minority and definitely negative, that contacted us as well. They were almost all fellow Christians.

We anticipated the negative reaction. First, you have to understand, this confession hit close to home. The average church and the average Christian have little to nothing to do with the poor or with HIV/AIDS, so when people acknowledge that ignoring poverty and turning a blind eye to AIDS is sinful, they must either acknowledge that truth or else neutralize it. Judging by the phone calls, many Christians were not about to let an indictment like this stick to them.

To give you an idea about how close the topic of poverty gets to home, consider Shane Claiborne's findings in a personal survey of people claiming to be strong followers of Christ, "I asked participants who claimed to be 'strong followers of Jesus' whether Jesus spent time with the poor. Nearly 80 percent said yes. Later in the survey, I sneaked in another question. I asked this same group of strong followers whether they spent time with the poor, and less than 2% said they did." [1]

In addition, a survey conducted by the Barna Group for World Vision in November 2002 found that only 3% of evangelical Christians would do anything to benefit an AIDS orphan. [2]

Please understand, we weren't confessing anyone else's sins. That was not our intention at all. The truth is that the vast majority of churches in America are guilty of these same things, and just hearing someone confess these issues as sinful indicts us all. We want to crucify the messenger rather than face the indictment.

(The most common objection to our ad was, "Shouldn't you have X used the money to help the poor?" I called this response the "Judas objection" because their question was an exact quote of what Judas said when he saw the woman breaking open the alabaster box of perfume to pour it out on the feet of Jesus (Matthew 26.9).

In that case, Jesus clarified what was really going on in the betrayer's heart. Judas didn't raise this objection because he cared about the poor. No, Judas' reason for voicing this objection was because he held the money and was selfishly pilfering from it to line his own pockets. It was selfish greed that was behind the objection, not genuine concern.

Most of the people who raised this objection, weren't doing so for the sake of the poor. They were doing it in an attempt to invalidate the apology. They, like Judas, held the moneybag and had no intention of turning loose of the purse strings so that real resources might flow toward the needy.

Now, I don't want to be dismissive of legitimate questions like, "Aren't there other ways to spend the money you spent for this ad, like in helping the poor?"

We acknowledge that every dollar given to the church is important. As a church, we spend far less than 1% of our annual budget on advertising every year. In fact, we have since cut out all advertising from our annual budget. To bring perspective, in the year that we apologized, we spent more than 30 times the amount spent on the ad in the form of relief to Africa, which did not include money spent locally on mission.

Consider this: Had I used our advertising budget to be self-promoting, as I had done for 16 years prior, no one would have even questioned our motives. Why not? We don't question those motives because we're used to churches spending money on self-promotion. In fact, in *The Dallas Morning News*, more than a dozen churches easily spend many times the amount we spent on our one-time ad for the advertisements they run every week. As long as you're telling the community that your church is the best thing since sliced bread, people will not object. Why do we find self-promotion acceptable and apologizing not?

There was one particular phone call that made me understand why our apology was so necessary. One week after the ad was placed, I told my wife that I believed that God had wanted to do a great good through the apology. I didn't know what, but I sensed from the moment God told me to publicly apologize that He intended to bring something truly good out of the event. While I knew I had done the right thing and many good things resulted, I wondered if I would ever really know in this lifetime what the greatest good was.

The conversation with my wife happened on a Friday afternoon. That same evening, we were out together on a date night when I received a call from the Bronx, New York. I knew no one in the Bronx. When the caller identified himself, he said, "This is David Miller. I'm on the board of the AIDS Institute and one of the original members of ACT UP NY."

He asked, "Are you the pastor that took out the ad in *The Dallas Morning News* apologizing for sitting on the sidelines while AIDS ravaged Africa?"

I told him, "Yes, I am."

He asked, "Is this for real?"

"Absolutely," I replied.

I explained how God had prompted me, how we had failed, and what we intended to do to live differently as a church. Miller then said, "Well, I've received no less than 1,000 phone calls and more than 300 emails asking me, 'Is this for real?' You see, those of us who work with HIV/AIDS have always said that we would love to have the church as an ally in this fight, but if the church were ever to join us in this fight, they first need to apologize for how they stood in the way for so many years. You're the first pastor in America to do that, and I'm calling to say thank you."

Well, by this point in the conversation, I was in tears. It was crystal clear why God wanted us to apologize. Not just because we had done wrong, which would have been reason enough, but because those who had been most hurt by the Church's actions really needed to hear our apology. They needed to hear an acknowledgement of wrongdoing from someone in the Church. Someone had to step up to the plate and own this failure without excuse. People who had been hurt needed to heal. This apology helped propel the healing process.

(The one thing I hoped for most was that those who had lost faith in ✗ the Church would dare to believe that a church could be known for its love and compassion more than its rhetoric and judgments.)

Because none of us can change the past, God has given us this glorious way of leaving the past forever in the past, through confession and the forgiveness that follows.

It is so extremely rare to ever hear a church apologize for anything it's done, but as a God-ordained, human-led organization, it regularly stands in need of forgiveness.

As a pastor, I have to model the values I want my congregation to live. If I preach reconciliation and forgiveness, but they never see me seek reconciliation and forgiveness, then they have reason to doubt just how much I really believe that which I preach. Personally, I would much rather be aligned with a church that can admit when it's wrong than the kind that never do.

In 1 John 1.9, John the Apostle wrote, *"If we claim to be without sin, we deceive ourselves and the truth is not in us! If we confess our sins, God is faithful and just to forgive us our sins and to cleanse us from all unrighteousness. If we claim we have not sinned, we make him out to be a liar and his word has no place in our lives."*

In truth, for that reason alone, an apology from a church should never "stand out." It shouldn't make the community sit up and take notice. It shouldn't be the big news of the day discussed in break rooms and over lunch. (But the apology does, and the reason the apology does is because the Church rarely does what it tells others to do.)

In all sincerity, we have to change and model correct behavior. The Church in America has a serious credibility problem. Those outside the Church look at us and often don't see anything that even remotely resembles Jesus. Instead, they see judgment, hypocrisy, and very little compassion. They hear our words but don't see a lifestyle that aligns with those words.

With this public apology, our foremost desire was to take responsibility for how we had failed. Secondly, in keeping with repentance, our desire is to keep our eyes on Jesus and stay focused on His mission. The only way the community will ever believe our words is if our behavior backs them up. With the help of God, we want to become a community of believers that lives out its creed.

My single biggest regret in the ministry is how I led my congregation for the first 16 years. I meant well, but nothing can change the fact that I was leading the Church the wrong way. I spent too many years not seeing what really matters, but I won't spend the balance of my life in that way.

These past several years have brought about a revolution in my church. We have been turned upside down and inside out. We are still far from perfect, but we are not the church we once were. The poor in our community and on the other side of the planet are our primary concern.

We are constantly learning and growing as we listen to God and listen to the poor.

As a result, a blue-collar church filled with plain old, ordinary people is helping to change the world. If my church can have a global impact, yours can too.

It was Henry Nouwen who said, "When we have been wounded by the Church, our temptation is to reject it. But when we reject the Church, it becomes very hard for us to keep in touch with the living Christ. When we say, 'I love Jesus, but I hate the Church,' we end up losing not only the Church but Jesus too." [3]

"The challenge is to forgive the Church. This challenge is especially great because the Church seldom asks us for forgiveness, at least not officially. But the Church, as an often fallible human organization, needs our forgiveness..." [4]

For many years, I've thought about what Nouwen said, "The challenge is to forgive the Church, but the Church seldom asks us for forgiveness." [5]

It's so true. I mean, think about it. How many times have you ever heard an official apology from a church? How about from your church? How many times have you heard an apology, apart from adultery, from a nationally known minister? How about from your pastor?

Let's look at the subject in another way. How often have you had to say you're sorry? How often in your marriage, on the job, or with your friends do you have to seek forgiveness, acknowledge a wrong, or admit fault? If you're anything like me, these happen often. Admitting my wrongdoing and saying I'm sorry is like taking out the garbage. I don't like to do it, but if I hang onto it, it stinks up the place.

We wouldn't get very far in life without apologies. In our brokenness, we mess up. We speak when we should listen. We hear things through our distorted filter and react to people based on woundedness. "You're right. I was wrong. Please forgive me," shouldn't be words we're unfamiliar with.

When we refuse to acknowledge the reality of our sin, we become what M. Scott Peck calls "people of the lie." [6]

9

You may successfully hide your messes from others, but the only one you're really hiding them from is yourself. The truth about Keith Stewart is this: I blow it. I make mistakes. I can misread a situation. I can believe I'm following God when I'm really only doing what I want to do.

It is simply not credible to think that a pastor or a church never would have a need to apologize, correct mistakes or acknowledge where things went wrong. It is simply unbelievable to have a pastor who never confesses or owns up to errors. It is also impossible that broken human beings, yes, even forgiven ones, don't need the power of confession to bring about the continued healing of that same brokenness.

With all of that said, I ask again, why is it that we seldom, if ever, hear the Church apologize for wrongs committed? It's like no matter what happens—church leaders take on the personality of politicians in the spin zone, focusing less on the wrong and more about how to save their reputation. When responsibility is deflected and excuses are made, people see right through them. Everyone knows how that game is played, because we've all played it.

Some church leaders go through life as if coated in Teflon, because no accusation, no lapse in judgment, and no fault ever sticks to them. Teflon is not good. Thomas Carlyle once wrote, "The greatest of faults… is to be conscious of none." [7]

Nothing ensures the demise of a leader more than the inability to admit fault. When rationalizations are always at the ready, and no accusation can penetrate his hardened outer shell, a leader has already sacrificed the ability to lead.

(Eugene Peterson's paraphrase of Romans 3.19 comes to mind: *And it's clear enough, isn't it, that we're sinners, every one of us, in the same sinking boat with everybody else.*)

The longer I walk with Christ, the more I live in touch with my brokenness. People in your churches may pedestalize you, but you've got to learn to take those kind words with a grain of salt. You are a spiritually flawed human being just like them. You are not the spiritual giant they believe you to be. You get it wrong. You have your struggles. You, like me,

are desperate for God to do in, through, and for you what you cannot do ⊗
for yourself. ⟩

If every human being is flawed, if every human being needs the disci-
pline of confession and churches believe that Christ followers need confession, then just like every other legitimate need, the church must lead
the way for the people. (Our congregation learns what is really important ✗
to us by the things we practice, not the things we say. If confession is necessary, truly indispensable, then the Church must show people how it's
done. The Church must lead the way.

We were wrong. We're sorry. Please forgive us. ⟩

Chapter 2

LOVE FUELS MISSION

W HEN I SHARE MY STORY with others, the thing they always remember is our apology to the community. Maybe it's because we're drawn to the dramatic, but in all honesty, to me the apology itself was anticlimactic. It was merely the next right thing to do. What is far more significant was all that transpired between my encounter with Oliver in the Soweto slum and the apology itself.

Once God opened my heart to the poor, the more I inclined my heart toward them, and the more God ratcheted up His communication with me. (God often speaks through the cries of vulnerable people.) X

My African journey took me next to Katito, a tiny region in Western Kenya. Katito is near Lake Victoria and fairly close to the Ugandan border. Largely populated by the Luo tribe, it's a pocket of humanity that is numbered among Kenya's poorest citizens.

World Vision had only been working in the community for a couple of years before I arrived in October 2006. As an outsider, my first impression was that there were many children and many elderly people, but hardly any young adults. Because the community shared a border with Uganda, the epicenter of the AIDS pandemic, and this community was poor, tribal, and largely uneducated, AIDS had spread like wildfire. This plague had eradicated most of the wage earners and community builders, leaving only the more vulnerable members of the community in its wake.

In this region of Kenya, besides the threat of HIV/AIDS, people were regularly dying of simple things such as diarrhea and other illnesses from drinking impure water. The lakes and streams in Katito from which the Luo get their water supply are often contaminated by livestock. Literally, these people were dying from a lack of clean water.

Without a doubt, the thing that got to me most on that first trip were the visits to child-headed households. A child-headed household is just that; in the event of the death of both parents, an older sibling becomes head of household, raising their younger brothers and sisters.

Other adults who live in the community also take ownership and responsibility for these child-headed households. On a regular basis, community members stop in to check on the children, ensuring they have food to eat and are going to school. If someone starts a business, there's always some way in which that business will use its goods or services to help provide for the widows and orphans in the community. I'd never seen a community working so cohesively together to solve what seemed like an insurmountable problem.

Even in the midst of some of the greatest need I'd ever encountered, I was struck by the love, faith, courage, and strong sense of community the people shared. America is one of the richest countries on the planet, but it's often quite poor when it comes to these same qualities. There among the poorest of the poor, I found great wealth. In fact, if you look at the comparison from God's perspective, the Luo of Katito have true wealth. They are rich in God's eyes.

Truthfully, I fell in love with the people I met. There was in my soul this sense that we were meant to be together. They were my missing piece, the direction I had lost, the something I was lacking. They were the answer to the question, "Is this worth getting up for?"

In the process, I discovered one of life's ultimate ironies: in depriving myself of relationships with the poor, I had impoverished my own life.

The truth is God hides His best treasures among the poor. The hand extended to you asking for help is often there to help you too. Remember the poor widow of Zarephath (1 Kings 17.7–16)? Little did she know that the stranger who came asking for bread and water would end up satisfying her hunger too. This reciprocity is the beauty and very nature of God's work. It is always mutually transformational.

Coming home from that trip left me with a lot to think about. All of these new thoughts and feelings needed some time to ferment. I had to hold them close, mull them over, and reflect on the truth I had received, so I resisted the urge to preach about it right away. I took three months just to seek God and ask for His direction. I didn't want my revelation to be another Band-Aid. If this was truly a new thing God was doing, it needed to be done right and needed to be done His way.

That three-month prayer pursuit was critically important because of the surprising discovery I made during that time. It's a conviction that over the past five years has only continued to grow. Here's my discovery: IT'S LOVE, NOT NEED, THAT FUELS MISSION.

You say, "Of course, Keith, everybody knows that."

I would say, "Almost everybody says that, but hardly anybody practices it."

Think about it. Practically every pastor who ever tries to mobilize his congregation in some sort of relief effort makes the appeal almost entirely by speaking about the need. Large charities working among the world's most vulnerable send out fundraising letters that detail the devastation caused by drought, famine, and other natural disasters. Nonprofits working in inner city neighborhoods will tell the story of the impact of record heat or record cold on the city's elderly and very young. The message is unmistakable: what these groups believe is that need is the primary motivator for action and giving.

There is an element of truth that need does drive impulsive giving. If something devastating happens in our community, or even halfway around the world, often Americans are immediately motivated to give or go. I love the response our country most often gives, but it is rarely sustained or lasts only as long as the particular need. Need-based giving tends to be short term, thus by nature it is reactionary.

Sustained commitment, giving that goes beyond the crisis, giving that is not reactionary or emotionally manipulated, requires more. It's love, not need, that fuels mission.

Mission is more. It's not crisis driven. It's relationally driven. It's not a gift but an investment. It goes beyond charity because it's Kingdom work.

On this side of the globe, as I contemplated what was so fundamentally life changing about this trip for me, I kept coming back to names and faces: Oliver, my inspiration from the Nairobi slum; Caroline, my five-year-old sponsor child whom I met for the very first time; Charles Kasura, a man who embodied compassion for his community; Richard Oppagala, a young driver brimming with leadership potential; and a teacher who walked for miles to take a thank-you note to a team member that had given her pencils and a packet of paper.

The needs in this tiny community were great, but what gripped my heart was love. Why did God knit our souls together? Frankly, because I needed them, and they needed me. I wanted to be rich where it counts like the Kenyans I'd met. My church in suburban Garland, Texas, needed the wealth found among the residents of Katito, too.

All I know for sure was this: No matter what we might ever do for them, the exchange between our two communities would always be lop-sided. We had money, but they had wealth. If they blessed us with their love, faith, courage, and community, we would be blessed indeed.

We all know the statistics:

- An estimated 2.1 billion poor people still lack access to safe water. [1]

- 4 billion of the world's poor live on less than $2 a day. [2]

- 6.9 million children under the age of five die each year from largely preventable causes. [3]

These numbers are huge, systemic and mind numbing, but they are not personal, and they never will become personal unless you have a love for just one of the millions represented by those numbers.

The truth is this: extreme poverty and human suffering must have a name, wear a face, and have an address.

Even more importantly, we must give our heart to someone in need. The Kingdom of God spreads in this way. It's why Jesus taught us the way of love: First, to love God with all our heart, mind, and strength, and second, to love our neighbor as ourselves.

Apart from loving my neighbor as I would my own flesh and blood, this revolution Jesus came to bring will never happen. Jesus put love at the center of mission.

So that was my dilemma. How do I bring a love revolution to my suburban church that bridges the chasm of an ocean, international borders, and cultural barriers? (If it's love and not need that truly fuels mission, then how was I to lead my people into loving the poor?)

Thankfully, World Vision had already provided the vehicle. The answer was child sponsorship. Years ago, when Bob Pierce started this amazing organization, it was a child in need that worked her way into Bob's heart that caused him to rethink missions. White Jade was her name. She was abandoned and needing sustained help. Someone had to be willing to make the sacrifice and provide for her. Bob did.

Through that experience, Bob Pierce became a facilitator of relationships like the one he had with White Jade. Through the organization he founded, World Vision would be a conduit to connect families in the developed world to orphaned and vulnerable children around the world.

The vision was pure genius and God inspired. With the investment of a little bit of money and a whole lot of love, lives were being changed on both sides of the globe, and change is really the main thing. (If it's God's work, done God's way, it will always be mutually transformational.) You and I are always as changed by the experience, as are those we help. If that's not happening, then it's either not God's work or else it's not being done in God's way.

I discovered my missing piece only after opening my heart to the poorest of the poor. The truth is my church needed these kids, even more than those kids needed sponsors. Our blinders had to be removed. We needed what these kids had never lost. If the investment of a little money and time in writing letters could produce just a fraction of what it was producing in me, then I knew that God could save us all.

As an aside, let me say that more and more leaders today are realizing (that relationships lie at the core of mission.) Most often, what they mean is their leaders have relationships with other leaders or those with the means to travel abroad can have these relationships, (but for the average person in their congregation, it's a proxy relationship, and it's not personal; thus, not really relational mission.)

The relational capacity of a missionary or pastor overseas is limited. He or she can only manage so many relationships with donors or sending churches. In practical terms, a handful of people have a relationship with those on the frontlines of mission. If you want mission to permeate your church, then as many people as possible need to have a personal investment in the mission.

Through child sponsorship, every single person in your church can have an individualized relationship with the field. The only limitation on that connection is self-imposed. How much is that individual willing to invest in writing letters and mentoring an orphaned child? Child sponsorship makes missional investment very real and very personal.

That's why we chose World Vision's sponsorship approach as our foundation. Whatever else lay ahead in our future, our congregation would no longer think in terms of the nameless, faceless poor. Statistics would trigger a far different reaction in those who knew someone represented by those mind-numbing realties. As our relationship deepened with Katito, all of us knew the names of those we were fighting for. They are like family to us.

Jesus once said, *"Where your treasure is, there will your heart be also"* (Matthew 6.21). Jesus was underscoring an undeniable spiritual connection between our wallets and our hearts. Where one goes, you will find the other. Treasure follows the heart; the heart follows treasure. They live in tandem.

If you want to see your church really give toward those in need, you'd better reach their hearts, and if you want to reach people's hearts, they need to fall in love.

As I said earlier, people don't really give in any kind of sustained way to need. Let's face it, if need were the principle driver in giving, then the organizations representing the neediest causes would always have the most money, but we know this not to be the case. People give in a sacrificial and sustained way where they have an investment of heart. It's love, not need, that drives mission.

In January 2007, three months after returning from Africa, I dedicated a month of Sundays to talking about the things I'd been learning and what God had been doing in me. At the end of the four-week message series, we planned a Hope Sunday. Hope Sundays help people under-stand what sponsorship is all about. Packets are prepared that list indi-vidual children who are available to be sponsored with background on their family and community.

On our first Hope Sunday, nearly every family at Springcreek ended up sponsoring a child. It was an amazing moment in time. But anybody can experience great moments in church. We wanted more. We wanted to see God ignite a movement. To us, the first Hope event was just a beginning, a great beginning, foundational stuff for sure, but God had greater intentions. Through relationships, God would begin molding Springcreek to have a heart more like His.

Sponsorship, having a relationship with a vulnerable child, is truly one of the most valuable relationships anyone can have in the Kingdom of God.

On my next trip to Africa, I travelled to visit with World Vision staff in Katito. I went with no agenda. For weeks before the trip, I prayed prayers of emptying, "God, relieve me of any expectations of what this trip should be for me or what it should produce in me. I want to be pres-ent to You, wherever I might encounter You. I have no plan but a desire to follow Your plan." Simply put, I wanted to listen and learn.

The moment I boarded the plane in Amsterdam for the final leg of my journey to Kenya, it became apparent to me that God would not disappoint.

I was seated next to a young woman name Veronicah Muthoni. She was born fifth of six children and abandoned by her parents on April 2, 1986, when she was just two years old. She was taken from the police station where she had been left to an orphanage called Blessed Hope Children's Center.

There I was, headed to Kenya in hopes of having a deeper experience of Kenyan life, and what does God do? He says, "I've arranged for you to be seated next to someone who grew up as an orphan child, and not just that, but a sponsor child. You can find out firsthand what that was really like for her." We talked for six and half hours of the eight-hour flight.

While at the orphanage, at age 5, it was discovered that Veronicah had a natural talent for singing that eventually became her contribution to the orphanage. She would direct choirs, write songs, and record albums to help raise money for the care of the other children. Veronicah was even asked to perform for Kenya's President Mwai Kibaki.

Sadly, this amazing young woman developed a hole in her vocal chords that Kenyan doctors said required surgery. Her sponsor parents, who lived in the Netherlands and were both in their 70's, managed to raise the money to fly Veronicah to the Netherlands to have the surgery.

Well, long story short, what she needed was vocal therapy to close up the hole and not surgery, which would require her to stay in the Netherlands with her sponsor family for two months while the doctors worked with her to help bring about the healing in her throat. The therapy worked with tremendous result.

One of the things I was most eager to learn was her perception of her sponsor parents before she had ever met them. She told me, "When I was young, even though I couldn't express it in words back then, I knew that somebody somewhere cared about me."

For the Veronicahs of this world, for those kids who've lost a mom or a dad, or sometimes both, sponsors are a lifeline. They are God's consolation in the midst of desolation that someone, somewhere cares. Relationships are THAT important to the work God is doing.

Think about it. If the one you thought you could count on your entire life was gone, taken from you, where would you turn? What choices would you make? Is it possible to overcome the wounding that type of loss would cause? Could a person growing up in those circumstances ever dare to believe that God could be good and never abandon them?

A sponsor's love made all the difference for Veronicah. She knew she was not truly alone in this world.

Veronicah had an extra-special blessing: she got to spend two months living with her sponsor family in the Netherlands. She had never met them before, nor had she ever been out of Kenya. She had never been on an airplane, never seen snow, never ice-skated, and never ridden a horse. She had never eaten lasagna (she loved it), pizza, hamburgers, ice cream, or waffles. She said she gained 7 pounds. She went to see her first movie and had never seen a bucket of popcorn so large and wondered if one person could eat it all. She found out that she could, and she did.

She had never had the experience of having a father. When I asked her if God had ever brought any men into her life while at the orphanage that were like a father to her, she sat there and pondered, remaining quiet for some time. When she finally broke the silence, she didn't talk about the orphanage. She talked about what the last two months had been like with her sponsor dad in the Netherlands.

She spoke of feeling loved and being treated like a cherished daughter. She had never had someone just want to do nice things for her, to give her life experiences she never had. The trunk full of gifts she'd been given by her family in the Netherlands was all headed back to Kenya with her to share with all the other children at the orphanage.

When I thought about what it would be like to go 25 years without a dad and to watch this young woman's face light up when she talked about her sponsor family made me realize just how important this work is that we're doing.

I wrote Veronicah's sponsor family in the Netherlands just so that they would know the life-changing effect they have had on this amazing young woman. They wrote me back, and this is what they said...

"You are right, she is a remarkable young woman, and precious in the eyes of God...We had such a blessed time the two months while she was here, but also it was not always easy for her. No, sometimes it was a big shock...we learned from her, as she learned from us...

"When you come from an area where you don't have a real toilet, only a hole in the ground that is shared with 50 other persons, not a cupboard, not your own bedroom, hardly anything of your own, and then you come into a total other world with all this luxury, your own room with a fireplace, with bridges in the streets, even main streets…for her it was hard to understand that this was possible and very normal. 'Everything was completely the other way,' she told us very often.

"One day when we asked her how she was thinking about our country, she said, 'it is a real wonderful world full of luxury and very nice people, I love it so, so, so, much, but…We Have More Fun…' We could understand her completely. Yes, they have so little, hardly anything, but they have each other and their belief in God our heavenly Father. We were very touched by her answer and loved her very much."

Poverty has become very personal to me. These people live in my heart. That's why I care because their stories now intertwined with mine, and their stories deserve to be told.

(Mother Teresa once said, "Let us not be satisfied with just giving money. Money is not enough, money can be got, but they need your hearts to love them." [4])

Dr. Martin Luther King, Jr., said something similar: "Pity may represent little more than the impersonal concern which prompts the mailing of a check, but true sympathy is the personal concern which demands the giving of one's soul." [5]

(Poverty must have a face and a name. We must feel the impact in relationship. Child sponsorship creates that vital link to a world of suffering.)

I must say if you have a heart for mission and you really want to see God move, not just in your leadership but also in every member of your church, then you must find ways to open up relationships with the poor to everyone. I'm not saying sponsorship is the only thing, or even that it should be limited to that, but those pathways must be made. I can tell you from personal experience that sponsorship opened up avenues of ministry that we never dreamed possible. When the people of Springcreek give, they speak of names, not needs. Isn't that what the Kingdom of God is supposed to look like?

Chapter 3

THE BLINDERS
COME OFF

O NCE OUR CHURCH EMBRACED THIS TINY, FORGOTTEN PART OF the world, things began to change. Without a doubt, our new-found friends had caused a shift in thinking that none of us anticipated. Poverty, which had been a largely taboo topic at our church, wasn't just coming up with greater frequency, but it was also beginning to define the types of conversations and messages we were having. Being in relationship with the poorest of the poor made us look at God's Word, His intentions for the church, and the part we play in it with far greater interest and intentionality.

What a radical shift from where we had been for years. Our people were accustomed to hearing messages about topics that they liked learning about: marriage, parenting, sex, work, and our personal relationship with God. Because poverty is not a "feel good" topic, it was largely avoided. In fact, the only time I had ever seriously addressed the issue was in a message series I called, "Stuff I Don't Want to Talk About." There were two messages in the series: "Poverty" and "Suicide." I shudder to think what I offered said about the state of my soul at the time.

We'd spent years training and conditioning our people to think that the church exists to meet their needs. As a result, once we shifted away from that selfish paradigm, backlash followed.

I had to own that; it was completely and totally my fault. That disgruntled element existed largely because of my poor leadership. I had taught them well, never in as many words, but by example, by sheer repetition, by avoiding topics that didn't play well to a seeker crowd. In truth, whether you're a seeker church or a more traditional church, we often send the unintended message to our congregations that church is all about them because the weekend services almost exclusively appeal to their preferences. It doesn't matter whether that preference is for an electric guitar playing the latest worship chorus from Hill Song or a pipe organ playing "Just as I Am," catering to preference is catering to preference.

Now, don't get me wrong, I always preached the truth, and I didn't entirely avoid saying the more difficult things that might not set well with a seeker crowd. But in choosing topics that people would find relevant, applicable, and personal, too much was being left unsaid. An issue such as poverty that literally saturates the Word of God was being treated like an unwanted stepchild.

Therefore, when I started speaking to the issue of poverty on a more frequent basis, the grumbling commenced. "Not Africa again," said the youth pastor. "I don't come to church to hear about Africa," came the response from another long-time family. And others voted with their feet as they walked out the door, never to return.

People didn't desert in droves. There was never anything even approaching a split in the church, but that some were walking away was unmistakable.

The purging that occurred over the next couple of years was necessary. Staff people who departed really needed to be someplace else. We were not going to be the church we once were. I would no longer be the church of "what's happening now" if that meant sacrificing what it meant to be God's Church. We had missed something vitally important. What was primary about the mission to which we were called was being sacrificed for secondary initiatives, which was now unacceptable.

Whether the message set well with a seeker crowd or not, we would no longer avoid the unpleasant topic of poverty. The road ahead for us had many challenges. Suburbanites, for the most part, have arranged their lives in such a way as never to have to regularly encounter poverty. In fact, we've carved out an existence that is comfortably isolated and insulated from the needs of the poor.

With our gated communities, privacy fences, and rear-entry garages, we barely know our neighbors, let alone those on the other side of town or in the inner city. We avert our eyes rather than look at the man who holds a sign and begs for money near the onramp to the freeway. We turn the channel rather than watch children in deplorable living conditions suffering with distended bellies. Our response is not good, not for the poor and not for us.

The sheer will power we exercise in avoiding the topic of poverty tells us how important it really is. If therapists saw the same level of avoidance in their clients, they would know that this was an issue that needed to be brought out into the open. Anything that is severely repressed and avoided suggests a deep underlying fear.

Fear? Fear about poverty? Why? There are at least a couple of significant reasons why we don't want to go there.

For one, poverty is troubling. Questions about the poor make us uncomfortable. It goes back to one of the oldest questions of humankind, *Am I my brother's keeper?* (Genesis 4.9b).

After Cain murdered his brother, God showed up and asked, *Where is your brother Abel?* (Genesis 4.9a). Of course, God knew exactly what had happened. An Omniscient Being never asks a question because He lacks information. God wanted Cain to own what he had done, to take responsibility for what he had caused.

But Cain refused to do so. Maybe he thought he was being clever. To him, his answer to God seemed to be the perfect excuse. *"Am I my brother's keeper?"* Although God never answered the question, the answer to the question is implied. "Yes, you are your brother's keeper."

Much like Cain, we're looking for the perfect excuse. We want something to say to ourselves that absolves us of our responsibility toward our brothers and sisters, and just like Cain, we provide only an elaborate ruse that aids us in our denial. But it doesn't work with God.

Poverty reminds us of our responsibility to our brother. We are far more interconnected than we realize or admit, which is especially true in the family of God. Though geography may separate us from one another, it doesn't relieve us of our responsibility toward our brothers and sisters. According to Scripture, if one part of the body suffers, every part suffers (1 Corinthians 12.26).

Poverty also reminds us of another even deeper reality that we deny. The poor in their outer condition mirror our inner condition. For this reason, poverty becomes personal and avoided like the plague–a graphic reminder of our own personal poverty.

Jesus' opening salvo in the Sermon on the Mount is a declaration that the blessed state begins in recognizing our spiritual destitution (Matthew 5.3). This is the price of admission to the Kingdom of God, a fundamental realization that when it comes to our actual condition before God, we are poor. The beggar's outer reality is our inner condition.

It's interesting that in the Greek language there are two primary words for "poor." (One word means you have just enough to get by, and the other means you have nothing at all.) The word used most often in the New Testament for "poor" is *penichros*. In one place, it's used to describe the widow who placed two small coins in the offering. Her resources were meager, but at least she had something.

When Jesus talked about our personal spiritual poverty, the word He used was for someone without any resources whatsoever, what we would term ("begging poverty." *Ptochos* literally means, "To cower and cringe like a beggar." [1] This word refers to the destitute. With this type of poverty, one's only option is to extend a hand to society, pleading for a handout.)

Jesus is saying, "The poor, those you think are in that condition because they deserve it, are being judged, or have squandered their opportunities...YOU are just like THEM." In fact, in many ways, our condition is far worse than theirs is. Their outer reality can be changed far more easily than our inner reality. To change our inner spiritual destitution—cost God His Son.

(To be "poor in spirit" means to recognize your true condition before God.) No matter how much effort we put into it, we can't scratch or claw our way out of this poverty. No one pulls himself out of spiritual poverty, and seldom does one admit their dependence on God. Instead, they go to great lengths to deny the reality.

(Because of our deep-seated denial, we can't stand any reminder of this truth. (For this reason, we avoid the poor like the plague.) (They remind us of our own vulnerabilities, brokenness, and powerlessness, so we keep the poor at arm's length, never allowing them into our hearts or lives.)

It's this lack of relationship with the poor that deprives us of something our souls need. The poor keep us tethered to the reality that we are truly interconnected (I am my brother's keeper) and that we are more alike than we are different (I share in their intrinsic poverty).

(Bottom line, we will never become the people God meant for us to be apart from a relationship with the poor. It's just not possible. We need them as much as they need us.)

In addition(as long as we avoid the poor, then ignorance, uninformed judgments, and stereotyping of them will flourish) It's far easier when the poor, in our minds, are lazy, undeserving, addicts, and criminals. We feel practically righteous in not helping people like that.(We say, "That would only further enable their irresponsible behavior.")

In the buckle of the ultra-conservative Bible Belt, people often subscribe to political positions that perpetuate the distorted notion that all poverty is a do-it-yourself job. This thinking is hopelessly out of sync with how God sees the poor and the reality of what is happening in society. Nonetheless, there were a good number of people within our church who held to such distorted thinking.

Therefore, beginning with children was the best way to bring about a revolution in the church. You see, people will never ask the hard questions about poverty (or even care) if we don't first learn to love someone who is in that state. Love will break open even the most hardened heart and prejudiced mind.

Regardless of the political narrative about the poor, those same things could not be said about children. Children have no control over the circumstances into which they are born. The children that World Vision made available to us had lost their parents and lacked access to water, education, and even the most basic of health services. They didn't fit into the convenient category of the undeserving poor. Their only crime was being born into poverty.(In opening up their hearts to these sponsor children, the church discovered a new openness and receptivity to God's truth about poverty.)

Then our excuses for noninvolvement evaporated. How could we say we truly loved them, especially in the way Jesus taught, "As we love ourselves," yet be willing to tolerate them living in scarcity while we lived in plenty?

For us, child sponsorship was the gateway to begin breaking down those barriers. Not only were the poor becoming a part of our world, but we were becoming a part of theirs as well. Relationship with them provoked all the right questions; Why are they poor? Why do we have so much when they have so little? What does it look like to truly help them?

Not only did this relationship help us see ourselves more clearly, but it gifted us with a new clarity in regards to God's Word. I'd read the Bible many times since I first met Christ, but all of a sudden it was like I was reading an entirely different book. From cover to cover, I was overwhelmed by the magnitude of verses concerning poverty. I realized the poor are integral to the story God is telling. A theology that dismisses them is not only in error but also hazardous to the soul.

If there were no other passages in the Bible except for this one I'm about to share with you, this one passage would be enough to underscore just how vitally important it is for the Church to reflect God's heart for the poor.

In Matthew's Gospel, Jesus unpacked His theology of the final judgment. In fact, there is no other place in the Gospels where Jesus says as much about the judgment as He does right here. He had some straightforward things to say...

> *When the Son of Man comes in his glory, and all the angels with him, he will sit on his glorious throne. All the nations will be gathered before him, and he will separate the people one from another as a shepherd separates the sheep from the goats. He will put the sheep on his right and the goats on his left.* (Matthew 25.31–33)

Clearly, this is the final judgment, and Jesus is speaking of a time of separation. Sheep will be separated from goats, but it's also here that the story takes an unexpected turn. Jesus is about to reveal the standard by which He can discern His sheep (the truly transformed) from the goats (those remaining in their old nature).

> *Then the King will say to those on his right, "Come, you who are blessed by my Father; take your inheritance, the kingdom prepared for you since the creation of the world. For I was hungry and you gave me something to eat, I was thirsty and you gave me something to drink, I was a stranger and you invited me in, I needed clothes and you clothed me, I was sick and you looked after me, I was in prison and you came to visit me." (Matthew 25.34–36)*

According to Jesus, providing the most basic of human needs like water, food, clothing, and caring for vulnerable people is the standard by which our lives will be judged. His sheep will have provided these needs while the goats will have not.

There's something within us that wants to object. Some of you are thinking, "But that sounds like I'm saved by my works." It may sound that way, but it's not. Christ is NOT saying that we're saved by our good works.

What He is saying is something far more profound. In the end, Jesus wants to know something besides whether you walked an aisle, said a prayer, or went to church. He's looking for evidence that grace has gripped your heart and transformed your life.

In the end, it's not "What have you done with Jesus?" but whether or not you have allowed Him to do anything in you, not "Did you pray a formulaic prayer?" but whether there is any evidence whatsoever that His presence in you has fundamentally changed your orientation toward the broken and needy in this world.

The evidence of a life transformed by God is liberation from the bondage of self-interest. It's the power of God alone that can set us free from the hoarding of resources and our over-consumptive lifestyles. At the heart of what it means to be a sinner is to be selfish, to want what I want. At the heart of what it means to be transformed by God is a new power to move away from selfish orientation and move in the direction of the best interests of others.

According to Jesus, my disposition regarding the most humble of life's essentials (water, food, clothing, and caring for the broken) is the most accurate barometer of whether or not God has transformed my life. Nothing else even comes close. Even the greatest of spiritual experiences cannot compare.

In another place, Jesus seems to anticipate this objection…

Many will say to me on that day, "Lord, Lord, did we not prophesy in your name and in your name drive out demons and in your name perform many miracles?" Then I will tell them plainly, "I never knew you. Away from me, you evildoers!" (Matthew 7.22–23)

Today we could voice similar objections, "But Lord, look at all these other amazing things I accomplished…I built a big church…we had a dozen campuses…we did amazing things on the weekend…people loved my sermons…"

Jesus is very clear on this issue: to succeed at everything else and fail at the test of the essentials is to fail utterly.

Jesus couldn't be any more explicit than this. We clearly know what He expects. We know because He said it. He made it plain, but many Christ followers have invented an entirely different scenario in their minds as to what will happen on the judgment day, a scenario that stands in bold opposition to the very words of Christ.

Those hearts that He occupies give evidence of His presence. He knows that when it comes to the most basic essentials of life, His kids will not only notice disparity, but they will be moved in their hearts to correct it, and they will, out of their resources, out of their own essentials… SHARE.

The heart that shares is the heart where Christ is enthroned. Jesus abides in the soul that sees the basic essentials of their life as opportunities to bless others lacking those same essentials. Christ takes up residence in generous hearts.

Thus, the work of God is better illustrated in a cup of water than a cathedral. It's more capably seen in a sack lunch given to the hungry than the slickest worship service. Its breathtaking beauty is put on display

34

more clearly in a coat given to the shivering homeless than the most gifted sermon offered on a Sunday. At least that's the way Jesus sees it.

Though I have been a Christian for more than 35 years and have served in full-time vocational ministry for more than 25 years, God is still saving me. He's still converting me. His work in me is intended to set me free from the prison of self-absorption and help me live with open hands and an open heart. I know I'm not yet where I long to be, but by the grace of God, I am not where I used to be, and I am eternally grateful that He set me on this journey and has been faithfully, patiently teaching me what matters.

Chapter 4

Our Love Affair with the Ways of Egypt

THERE ARE REALLY <u>THREE TYPES</u> of <u>apologies</u>.

(First, there are the people who are sorry because they've *1.* been caught.) Often these apologies are accompanied by big crocodile tears and seemingly endless remorse, but in truth, the contrition lasts only about as long as the spotlight on their sin does. We've all known people like this, maybe even ourselves.

(Secondly, there are the people who are sorry because they were *2.* wrong, and they know it.) Admittedly, that's a big improvement over the former apology. It is important for people to be able to name the wrong they committed and own it without excuse or blame. We usually don't expect anything more, and typically, it's as good as it gets.

(There is a third type of apology that goes one step further. This apol- *3* ogy is one that acknowledges wrongdoing without blame or excuse, but in addition says, "I'm sorry for what I caused.") What separates these people from the ones who merely acknowledge wrongdoing is that they are truly broken, and (because they are broken over their sin,) they not only *X* see it clearly, but in addition, see and own the repercussions. Broken people understand that no one sins in a vacuum, but that others are hurt by their failures. The broken will own the resultant fallout from their sins.

In other words, they acknowledge, ("Because I did wrong, I hurt oth- *My wife* ers,) and I've caused them to perceive me in a different way." One of the *with my* *lock of* most damaging things about personal failure, when we sin, is we damage *income* trust. We sacrifice a measure of believability, and our credibility is called into question.

It's interesting that the words "credit" and "credo" (a statement of one's beliefs) come from the same root. When retailers check your credit score, what they're really doing is checking how much believability you have accrued. Before they trust you with credit, they want to know how well you have kept the promises you made to other merchants.

It's no different for us. When people watch and listen to us, they are doing thousands of little credit checks. They are constantly monitoring whether or not they believe us based on prior things we've said or done.

When we sin, we damage our credit score with others. Our believability always takes a hit. People are more cautious with us, and trust is fragile. They ask more questions. They are slower to commit to us. They have to re-evaluate the relationship. All of which is perfectly understandable and expected. It's what normal people do.

When broken people own their failings, they don't insist on being believed by those they've failed. The truly broken aren't constantly asking, "When are you going to get over that and let it go?" People who are genuinely penitent are patient with others damaged by their sins. They know the only way to win them over is not just with meaningful words but also with meaningful actions.

Once Springcreek admitted we were wrong, the spotlight was turned on us. Would we live like a church that knew it made mistakes, led people down the wrong path, and sincerely wanted to do life and ministry differently? Would we take ownership over what we had caused? These are all legitimate questions. People would be watching our lives to determine the truth.

After placing the ad, I spent the next six weeks teaching the church in what specific ways we had blown it. It was very important for all of us to be on the same page. Our members needed to hear their leader articulate what compelled us to apologize to the community.

Confession is such an interesting word. Literally, in the original Greek, the word means, "to say the same thing." In a very real sense, that's what confession does. It says the same thing about our sin that God does. When I confess, I agree with God about the nature of the wrong.

Today, even four years after the apology, my mind still goes back to that event as a kind of watershed moment in the life of our church. With the watchful eye of our congregation and community upon us, we had an opportunity to be different.

The main reason why any apology must be sincere and not a gimmick is people will call you out on it. Your credibility in the eyes of many will be damaged. If you aren't ready to own what you caused, then you're not ready to apologize.

We are not yet what we long to be, but, thank God, we are not where we were. Without a doubt, one of the biggest reasons for creating the mess we had created stemmed from listening to the wrong authorities. Please, don't misunderstand me. What I did was my fault. It didn't matter what anyone else was saying or doing; I made my own choices. As a part of my fouled-up decision-making process, I spent more time listening to the leaders of big, successful churches than I did listening for God's personal leadership in my life.

Conferences can be challenging. They can be informative and inspirational, or they can be a source of temptation for pastors. If being successful or having a growing church becomes too important to you, then you will spend most of your life compulsively chasing after the next new thing. Pragmatism (what works versus what's right) will become your guiding principle for ministry, and people will be valued only for their usefulness in moving you toward your goals.

None of what I'm saying is meant to be an indictment against the churches that constantly host conferences or the men that lead them. I'm not saying that these are the principles they operate from. I'm just saying that for me that is what conferences became.

I had over-empowered the wrong voices in my life. Now for several years, Springcreek has been getting back to the basics. It was clear where we had jumped the tracks. If God's voice had been drowned out by others, it was time to get back to listening to Him and His Word.

Getting it wrong in such a significant way made me realize there was one mistake I fully intended never again to replicate. I don't care how "successful" another church or pastor is; they are not worth following. I would rather imperfectly follow God's leadership for me than perfectly imitate someone else's success.

This apology resulted in a genuine and much needed renewal in my relationship with God. Even within the church, there was a growing appetite for more of God. In retrospect, it is so clear to me now. God was preparing us for a new adventure, something unlike anything we'd ever experienced before. In the past, we had relied on our own creativity and ingenuity to get us where we wanted to be. Now we were being called to places where God wanted us to be, requiring only what God could give.

It's laughable that any of us thinks we can lead without sending deep roots into Christ, but in the ministry, the demands are so high and the time so limited, our lives quickly fill with activities. The demands never stop, and there's always one more thing to do. Prayerlessness is the secret sin of the average American pastor. They are doers and achievers but typically not contemplatives. (The soul work they need is constantly shoved to the side in the name of getting stuff done.)

When the pastor does pray, it's usually in public or on the run or for a special need. However, the kind of praying a pastor needs is soaking prayer where he simply lingers in God's presence, prayer that reminds him that it's not all about him but all about God. If a pastor isn't getting quality "God time," he will die on the vine. It happened to me. It can happen to you.

Our capacity to do the work of ministry is very limited, but to do the work of God in our own strength is impossible. What God wants done in the world takes the resources He provides. Those resources are only found in Him. They cannot be accessed in books, and they can't be taken home in a goody bag from the next conference. (There is no substitute for time with God.)

(There are two things I know beyond a shadow of a doubt about leaders: They can't teach what they don't know, and they can't lead where they won't go.)

There was an unmasking of our church that continued to unfold. I didn't like the things I was discovering. After a couple of staff transitions,

(I was shocked to discover the complete lack of discipleship going on in our adult ministries.)

I was in a meeting with the coaches in our small group ministry and talking about spiritual growth — how it occurs, what is God's part, what our part is, and what we do as leaders to facilitate it. After more than an hour of engaging conversation, I asked these leaders, "How much time in the last three years have you spent talking about matters like these?"

"Zero," they answered in unison.

"Wait a minute," I said, "If you haven't been talking about this kind of stuff, what have you been discussing?"

"Systems and structure," was the answer.

"Then, as coaches, what do you do?" I asked.

They said, "We spend about half our time explaining how the structure changed this month and the other half of our time dealing with problem people."

As much as I would like to scapegoat on the pastors who were their leaders, once again, the fault lie with me. The practice was going on under my nose, and I was disengaged enough from adult ministry not to be aware of the total lack of spiritual training our people were receiving.

Our process was a mess. Understand, it wasn't a new mess. It had been a mess for some time, and I was just becoming aware of it. But it was really just par for the course. When you make your goal increasing numbers as some sort of barometer of church success, then what matters most are ways to count and track those numbers. Our practice synced perfectly with our values. We had systems people, not disciple makers.

I'm not saying that systems are unimportant. They are very important, but they are not of first importance. (Of first importance is to know what you are trying to produce and how that happens.) To be incredibly efficient at producing nothing is still producing nothing.

Having made this discovery sickened me to no end. I thought, "God, I know we were wrong, but were we really that wrong? Were we getting anything right?"

To be honest, after what we had been through already, this revelation nearly pushed me over the edge. I wanted to quit. I was thinking,

"We're in such a deep hole and have lost so much ground and time, can we ever dig out of this mess?" But I couldn't get past the fact that this is what I had caused. It was one thing to say I was wrong; it was another thing entirely to own the mess I made. It wouldn't have been right for me to abandon ship, not right then knowing what I knew.

I took a couple of months to pray about how I needed to respond. It became apparent to me during that time that in the same way we owned getting so much else wrong, we needed the same type of ruthless honesty now. We were going to have to teach and lead our way out of this mess, but I needed to get a baseline understanding of where we really were. To get the Titanic turned around, I needed to start with those at the helm.

I'll never forget the staff meeting when I sat down with the pastors and explained, "I need to know where you are with God. I promise you, this won't affect your job or my opinion of you, but I need your complete and total honesty. How's your walk with God? How close and connected do you really feel to Him? Do you hear Him speak to you? Do you understand what's involved in leading others into a growing relationship with Christ? If you don't, that's okay. I can teach you what you don't know. However, if you pretend with me now, you won't move on, you'll just stay stuck. You won't grow except in your capacity to deceive yourself and others. No matter where you find yourself, we can improve on it. The only thing that will keep you from getting what you need is the fear of looking like a beginner. If you can overcome that fear, we can grow together."

It was exactly what our staff needed — permission to be real, open, and honest about their struggles and shortcomings. Over the next several months, in an environment of honesty, encouragement, and teaching, we grew together. As we restored the centrality of our walk with God, gradually we began to move away from a business mentality for ministry to embrace Christ's model for ministry. The single most important thing I do as a pastor is belong to Jesus. That's job one. If I fail at that and succeed at everything else, I am an utter failure.

In that time, I came across an older work by Eugene Peterson called, *Working the Angles*. In the opening pages of his book, he described to a "T" what our church had become.

"American pastors are abandoning their posts left and right, and at an alarming rate. They are not leaving their churches and getting other jobs. Congregations still pay their salaries. Their names remain on the church stationary, and they continue to appear in pulpits on Sundays. But they are abandoning their posts, their calling. They have gone whoring after other gods. What they do with their time under the guise of pastoral ministry hasn't the remotest connection with what the church's pastors have done for most of twenty centuries.

"A few of us are angry about it. We are angry because we have been deserted…It is bitterly disappointing to enter a room full of people whom you have every reason to expect share the quest and commitments of pastoral work and find within ten minutes that they most definitely do not. They talk of images and statistics. They drop names. They discuss influence and status. Matters of God and the soul and Scripture are not grist for their mills.

"The pastors of America have metamorphosed into a company of shopkeepers, and the shops they keep are churches. They are preoccupied with shopkeepers concerns — how to keep the customers happy, how to lure customers away from competitors down the street, how to package the goods so that the customers will lay out more money." [1]

The language of Zion has changed. Churches have morphed into business empires, complete with image, product, branding, and bottom lines. Our church was rapidly becoming just like that until God interrupted. Thank God for that work He started in me while standing in a slum on the other side of the world; once again, the poor were helping to save our church.

Let me tell you something I learned from the people of Katito that became so incredibly valuable to me during this time of rebuilding. The people of Katito live very connected to the land, very close to the soil. Seemingly a very small thing, but it's a small thing with major implications.

We, as Americans, for the most part, no longer live connected to the land. Food for us doesn't come from a field; it comes from the grocery store. Our water is not from lakes and rivers; it comes out of pipes in our homes, and if we want a drink, it comes from a bottle in the store.

Obviously, I'm overstating to make a point, because we really do know that the water comes from rivers and lakes and reservoirs, and we know that our vegetables were grown in fields, but we don't really live connected to that reality like a farmer does, especially not like a Kenyan farmer. For example, when I listen to my Kenyan friends talking about rain, everyone is happy. Kenyans thank God for the rain because they know they need it to grow crops, and that's what brings them food. They thank God for the rain He brought.

There is thankfulness because they still think like the Bible does, that rain is a good thing. For example, when the Bible says, *God causes his rain to fall on the just and the unjust* (Matthew 5.45), they understand that verse. It's a positive statement. It's saying, "God sends good things on just and unjust people," because rain is a very good thing.

In our culture, we don't ever use that verse that way. When we quote this verse, it's because something bad has just happened, so we say, "Well, you know, it rains on the just and the unjust." In our mind, rain is a negative thing. We complain about rain because it spoils our plans to be outside. The only time we're thankful for it is when we get a break from big utility bills to keep the grass green. We use this verse to say, "No one is exempted from the bad stuff."

It's because of this connection to the land that the Kenyans understand that God is the provider of rain. God sends the good rains that produce the crops that feed our families. As a result, they also express their gratitude more openly and frequently. They pray over every meal, and they pray over morning and afternoon tea; they pray and thank God for everything.

There's even more to their reality than that. The poor have taught me something about the nature of the work of God itself. You see, the average Kenyan is a dry-land farmer because irrigation for crops is not available everywhere in Kenya.

Numerous farmers make full use of irrigation methods, but most are simply not close enough to rivers or water sources to have that as an option. What that means is they are absolutely dependent on God for rain. Dry-land farmers are, by definition, very dependent on the rain to come in its season.

Did you know this dependency is a big deal in the Bible? When the children of Israel were finally liberated after 400 years of Egyptian bondage, God began to prepare them for a new reality. Something about Canaan would be dramatically different from Egypt. To be sure, it was a land flowing with milk and honey, but this land would be different from Egypt in a far more significant way than just that. Listen to God describe this new reality...

> *The land you are entering to take over is not like the land of Egypt, from which you have come, where you planted your seed and irrigated it by foot as in a vegetable garden. But the land you are crossing the Jordan to take possession of is a land of mountains and valleys that drinks rain from heaven. It is a land the Lord your God cares for; the eyes of the Lord your God are continually on it from the beginning of the year to its end. So if you faithfully obey the commands I am giving you today — to love the Lord your God and to serve him with all your heart and with all your soul — then I will send rain on your land in its season, both autumn and spring rains, so that you may gather in your grain, new wine and oil. I will provide grass in the fields for your cattle, and you will eat and be satisfied.* (Deuteronomy 11.10–15)

Do you hear what He's saying? Egypt was a land of farming technology. They had modern irrigation methods even back then. Irrigation is a great thing, right? I mean, it helps you be more in control of the development of the crop and when the harvest comes. But God said, "This land of abundance where I am taking you is a place where you will be utterly dependent on Me for the rain in its season."

What does all of this talk about rain have to do with ministry? It has a lot to do with ministry. Consider this: which is God's work most like, Egypt or Canaan?

Being among my farming friends in Katito opened my eyes to read the Bible with a new perspective, that of a dry-land farmer who is completely and totally dependent on God. Scripture constantly borrows metaphors from agriculture to describe the work of God. The Bible talks about fields that are white unto harvest, the Lord of the harvest, and God sending rain on the just and unjust. It talks about planting and watering and how God and only God can make the seed grow.

The truth is technology and modern methods can be a good thing, and we like to make full use of these things in ministry, but sometimes we become so dependent on the ways of Egypt that we forget who the real Provider of blessings is. We start thinking like many Americans do today, that my food comes from the store and my water from these pipes. We depend so much on ourselves that we forget the Lord of the Harvest.

The Bible underscores the fact that ministry is more like Canaan than it is Egypt. All the technology and methodologies of Egypt cannot change the human heart. The things that need to happen in our people's hearts, in their lives, in their decisions, in their wallets, in their priorities, you and I are powerless to make happen. The methodologies of Egypt are not the engine of ministry.

It's like Marilee Dunker Pierce, Bob Pierce's daughter, once said, "There's a great tsunami flowing, and we didn't CREATE it and we don't SUSTAIN it, but we can RIDE it." [2]

Jesus said, *"Apart from me, you can do nothing"* (John 15.5). I carry in my heart every day the reality that in this business, we call the work of God that I am a dry-land farmer like my friends in Katito. I am absolutely dependent on God to show up, bring the rains, and bring the harvest.

I agree that technology and many modern methods can be good things. They can aid us in our communication and help us better tell His story. What I am saying is not anti-technology any more than it is anti-irrigation. But just like He did with His people in the Old Testament, God is reminding us of a reality that we sometimes forget: He is Lord of the harvest, the supplier of the blessings. If hearts are to be changed, if lives are to be transformed, it's because He has done it, not us.

God started a revolution at Springcreek that went well beyond becoming externally focused. Through the poor, we were reminded to send our roots deeply into Christ. Because of relationship with them, God's truth opened to us in new and exciting ways. Our eyes were opened to see the things we'd been missing.

I thought I was going to Africa to save them. I know now that God was bringing Africa into my life to save me.

Chapter 5

POVERTY IS
A JUSTICE ISSUE

I MENTIONED EARLIER HOW MY TIME in God's Word profoundly changed. It was now like I was reading an entirely different book. In loving the poor, something shifted in my understanding and made me want to see life from their perspective.

At best, I confess, I am extremely limited in my capacity to do this. For one thing, I am not materially poor. In our society, though there are millions who make more than I do, when compared to the world's poor, I am numbered among the very rich. The other reason I am so limited is I have a position of power and influence as a pastor and community leader. I experience most of life from the top side of power and not from underneath it. It would be the utmost arrogance on my part to say I really see life from the perspective of the poor.

So what I must do is:

- Acknowledge my limitations.
- Listen well to the poor.
- Seek God who sees life perfectly from all perspectives.

The Bible was written from the perspective of the underside of power. Few books in history share this amazing quality. Instead, books are often written by the world's winners and conquerors with a bias toward seeing history from their skewed perspective. Consider just this one example: the story of the founding of our own country is told one way through our American History textbooks and very differently from the perspective of Native Americans. The conqueror tells the story differently from the conquered.

The Bible is the narrative of God told from the vantage point of those under power. It's the story of God forming a people unto Himself, a people who spent generations enslaved, persecuted, and martyred. They were a people who knew the bitter taste of poverty and the oppressive nature of powerful nations who held them in their grip. When they tell their story, it's with the acute awareness that they have known the boot heel applied to the neck more often than they've known the crown atop their head.

It's very difficult for many of us to make this shift, to see life from the bottom up versus the top down. It doesn't come naturally when all we have ever known is a life of privilege, wealth, and power. As a society, we have been given many breaks that others have never received. Again, let me repeat, we often compare ourselves to others within our own society, so we don't think of ourselves as having great wealth and privileges, but according to the Global Rich List website, if you make an annual salary of $25,000, you are numbered in the top 10% of wealthiest people on the planet. [1] That's not to discount poverty within our own country, but to try to help us keep things in perspective about the abundant wealth that many of us possess, although we may not see it that way.

X (If I am to understand God's Word, a shift in perspective must first take place. I can't read the Bible from a top-down point of view. It must be read as it is written, from the bottom up.) This perspective may seem like a small issue, and it is, but it's a small issue with huge implications.

In addition, I have to be aware of my own propensity to rationalize those areas where I am disobedient. I can tell you first hand that for a good number of the Scriptures we'll be looking at, I had alternate explanations. Certainly, there is always room for a different understanding and interpretation in many Biblical passages, but the common denominator in all of my alternate explanations was that they let me off the hook. Rationalization suggests something other than scholarly debate and something more akin to excuse making.

What I had to learn to do is sit with a passage and let it say what it says. I had to resist the urge to find some way to explain away the fact that I failed to live it. It is unsettling to be measured against a truth and come up lacking. The word for my resistance is dissonance.

The verses in the Bible that remind us of our responsibility to the poor often create this feeling of dissonance. When what we think and how we live do not agree, the result is disharmony. These verses throw a wrench into the works. The gears were all working just fine, like a well-oiled machine, and then along came an inconvenient truth, and suddenly, "BAM," everything ground to a halt.

Most all of us have such a low tolerance for dissonance that we try to rid ourselves of this uncomfortable feeling as quickly as possible. To do so means either aligning our actions with our thinking or revising our thinking to fit our actions. In this context, we either bring our lives into conformity with God's thinking (His Word) or else we modify our thinking so that there is no longer a conflict.

Given the choice between the two, when how I actually live is significantly at odds with what God has said, I have often found a convenient rationalization. The easy way is to play an intellectual game with myself by figuring out some way the verse I'm reading doesn't apply to me. I have played this game far too long. I would rather acknowledge my disobedience, asking God for the willingness and power to do as He says, than engage in my ongoing, desperate machinations to circumvent the truth.

I'm not going to pretend with you; some of the stuff that I will share is going to create dissonance. It did with me. I can't prevent that from happening, nor do I desire to prevent it. The wrestling match you are about to undergo is worth it. Dissonance is the catalyst God uses to propel us forward.

Believe me, God and I have wrestled into the night on many occasions as a result of these verses. They afflicted me. They mucked up the comfortable life I had carved out for myself. I was wrecked in all the ways I needed to be wrecked, so in the remaining chapters, I won't be doing a comprehensive treatment of all the Bible verses related to poverty; it's simply my desire to walk through some of the primary passages that concern our relationship to the poor. In so doing, I hope to demonstrate to you that our responsibilities to vulnerable people permeate every aspect of Scripture.

Before my encounters with the poor of Katito, Kenya, I had been living with my eyes half shut. Not only was I not seeing the poor, but I was not seeing the central role they play in Scripture.

God's word has so much to say about the poor and poverty. The sheer number of verses is overwhelming. Consider Rich Stearns and Lamar Vest's observation, "Despite the fact that God's heart for the poor is mentioned in some 2,100 verses of Scripture, many of us simply miss it. In a recent survey of adults in America conducted by Harris Interactive, although 80 percent of adults claimed to be familiar with the Bible—the best-selling book in history—46 percent think the Bible offers the most teachings on heaven, hell, adultery, pride or jealousy. In fact, there are more teachings on poverty than on any of those topics." [2]

Even more important than the number of verses related to poverty is the message contained in those 2,100 verses.

The Bible gives us more than 20 different causes of poverty. The explanations run the gamut from laziness to misfortune. Without a doubt, the biggest mistake people make in reading the Bible is zeroing in on one explanation to the exclusion of all others. As a result, a relatively minor cause of poverty becomes THE explanation for all poverty.

In our culture (and sometimes in the church) that default explanation is laziness. Many are quick to blame poverty on the behavior of the poor, but in truth, some of it is the direct result of the unwillingness to work. Scripture says as much.

In Proverbs 6.6–11, Solomon talks about the sluggard and the poverty that overtakes him. We're reminded that *lazy hands… lead to poverty* (Proverbs 10.4). In another place, we're told *… the one who loves sleep… grows poor* (Proverbs 20.13); and *whoever loves pleasure will become poor* (Proverbs 21.17). Pretty strong evidence, right?

I admit if all we had in the Bible were these explanations, we'd be forced to conclude that poverty is a "do-it-yourself" job. Certainly, I'm not denying that the behavior of the poor does account for a certain percentage of poverty that exists in the world. But is that the extent of Biblical wisdom on this issue? Hardly!

Political pundits, however, often get a great deal of mileage out of this accusation. They tap into our deeply rooted American ethic of the rugged individualist who pulls himself up by his own bootstraps. We reason, "If you're poor, you must be lazy or not doing enough." Or else we say, "Everyone has the same opportunities in this country. If you didn't take yours, you must be unwilling to work."

Someone once said, "We don't really live in a democracy. We live in a meritocracy." In other words, we believe people always get what they deserve, so when it comes to poverty, we assume the poor must have brought this condition on themselves.

We have to remember two things.

First, the pull of our culture is constantly away from a view of reality that reflects God's truth. To lump all the poor into the category of the lazy and unproductive is a politically expedient position that is Biblically ignorant. God calls on us as Christ followers to think differently rather than simply merge our thinking with the cultural stream. We're compelled to ask ourselves if laziness accounts for some poverty, is it fair to lump all of the world's poor into this category? The answer from God's Word is a resounding "NO!"

By the way, the next time you're tempted to offer laziness as the best explanation for poverty, remember what Pharaoh said to the children of Israel when they complained about being forced to make bricks without straw.

> *Pharaoh said, "Lazy, that's what you are—lazy! That is why you keep saying, 'Let us go and sacrifice to the LORD.' Now get to work. You will not be given any straw, yet you must produce your full quota of bricks." (Exodus 5.17–18)*

Ruthless, godless leaders making irrational demands of the people they oppress gravitate toward this explanation of poverty. It's easy to accuse people of laziness while ignoring the fact that we've stacked the deck against them. Accuse and ignore is what depravity does best. It puts people into no-win situations and then blames them for the failure.

Second, we need to remember that laziness is offered as an explanation for poverty a total of nine times in Scripture. Certainly, if the Bible says something once, it is important. I am not debating the importance of biblical repetition, but it's worth considering that there are other explanations for poverty that occur far more frequently in Scripture. In my opinion, these other explanations constitute a much better explanation for the magnitude of poverty that exists in our world. In addition, these other explanations are literally woven into the fabric of hundreds of Bible stories.

Related to this argument that ties poverty to the behavior of the poor is the suggestion that the poor have too many children. Maybe that's why they're poor. Honestly, this argument was once a big prejudice of my own. I questioned why families in the developing world had so many kids. In my mind, I thought, "No wonder you struggle."

Consider this scenario: how many children would you have if you knew that half of your kids would die before reaching the age of five and half of the remaining half would die from other preventable diseases before they reached the age of eighteen?

How many kids would you have if you knew that your male offspring would be your only source of security for the future? How large would your family be if children were your only source of help if you got sick? What if your children were the only ones who could fetch water when you couldn't or work the plow when you're bedridden? How many kids would be enough if they were your only life insurance, medical insurance and retirement? Without children to pitch in and help during a time of need, a bad case of diarrhea could threaten not just an individual's health but reduce his entire family to destitution.

It's easy to parrot explanations about the root causes of poverty while living in isolation from the suffering of more than half the world's population. Far too many of us know all the answers before we've even understood the questions. Of course, the main reason we cling to unthinking answers is because as long as we define all or most poverty in this way, we can justify washing our hands of the issue. Willful ignorance does not absolve us of our responsibility toward the poor. Lumping people together as the "undeserving poor" is something God sees right through.

Remember that in the same wisdom literature where Solomon speaks of laziness, he also says...

Those who shut their ears to the cries of the poor will be ignored in their own time of need. (Proverbs 21.13)

And...

The godly care about the rights of the poor; the wicked don't care at all. (Proverbs 29.7)

Solomon makes clear that whatever exemption we've created for ourselves will not wash with God, and certainly Solomon is implying in these verses that there's a type of poverty that is not self-induced and requires our involvement and advocacy.

What other explanations does the Bible offer for poverty? Whereas many want to lay the greatest blame for poverty on the behavior of the poor, the Bible suggests an alternate explanation, that poverty is something that's been done TO people.

In fact, there's an entire book in the Old Testament that tells the story of a righteous man reduced to poverty. His name was Job, and his poverty was the direct result of a series of calamities brought on his life by the enemy.

Misfortune accounts for a lot of poverty in the world today. Famine, drought, hurricanes, tornadoes, earthquakes, illness, fire, and death are all major players in creating poverty or the condition through which poverty eventually comes. These natural and sometimes man-made disasters don't discriminate in their decimation. They are equal-opportunity destroyers. When disaster strikes, vulnerable people often lose everything, precarious economies are destroyed, and hope for a rapid turnaround is all but lost.

(Related to life's misfortunes are three categories of people who get maximum exposure in the pages of Scriptures. They are the widow, the orphan, and the alien. In the Old Testament and New Testament alike, these are the three most mentioned categories of people in the Bible.)

So what, if anything, do the three have in common?

A widow? A woman who lost her husband.

An orphan? A child that lost their parents.

An alien? A foreigner who had lost his home and was forced to migrate to a new country in order to survive.

Each one had been the victim of misfortune. Each one was in some way vulnerable. Each one had suffered some sort of loss beyond their control. Each one had either been plunged into poverty or teetered on the edge of it, and each one could be easily overlooked because everyone who cared about them is gone. They've lost parents, spouses, and community.

Old and New Testaments remind us of our special obligation to help this special class of vulnerable people.

> *Religion that is pure and undefiled in the eyes of God the Father is this: to take care of widows and orphans and remain unstained by the world.* (James 1.27)

> (God) *... defends the cause of the fatherless and the widow, and loves the alien, giving him food and clothing.* (Deuteronomy 10.18)

In life, bad things happen that leave vulnerable people in their wake, and during these times, the churches God approves of, are the ones who care for those affected by life's tragedies, not the one that judges them.

Once again, from the wisdom literature, Solomon says in Proverbs 14.21, *It's criminal to ignore a neighbor in need, but compassion for the poor—what a blessing!*

When your neighbor is in need, God calls for redemptive action on your part. Not only is assisting necessary, but according to Solomon, not to help is criminal. In other words, it is so unethical in the eyes of God that it actually transgresses His sacred laws.

Even though misfortune is a far more plentiful explanation than pinning the cause of poverty on the behavior of the poor, there is yet another explanation in the Bible that is offered even more frequently. In fact, this explanation occurs at a ratio of 50 to 1 to any other cause.

To have a truly Biblical view of poverty, you have to understand that the taproot of most poverty is oppression.

To have a view of poverty that fails to account for oppression is to have a non-biblical view. In fact, I'll go even further and say that we'll never have God's heart for the poor as long as we fail to understand how pervasive oppression really is. Oppression wears many faces in Scripture. It is imperative that you learn to recognize those faces because little has changed in the 2,000 years since the Bible was written.

To give you an overview of how pervasive this explanation of poverty really is, simply type in the word "oppress" into a Bible search engine on the computer. While the list generated will not list every example of oppression in the Bible (just where the word "oppress" actually occurs), you will discover a thread that is woven into the very fabric of Scripture.

It begins during Israel's defining moment, 400 years of Egyptian slavery, which the opening chapter of Exodus described in this way: So they put slave masters over them to oppress them with forced labor, and they built Pithom and Rameses as store cities for Pharaoh. (Exodus 1.11)

Years of oppression under Egyptian rule reduced Israel to extreme poverty, and while Israel's wealth was plundered, along with her strength, Egypt was made incredibly wealthy, so much so, that in the verse referenced above, Israel was being forced to build two entirely new cities just to store Egypt's excess wealth. This single verse is a stunning revelation about what really lies behind oppression: Greed. This insatiable desire for more caused Egypt to rob generations of families of their rights and resources so that they could get rich at others' expense. Keep Israel's plight in mind, because Pharaoh's dynamic plays out in more ways than one.

After years of systemic oppression, God permitted the Israelites to plunder their captors before leaving Egypt because the Egyptians had taken what did not belong to them in the first place. The Egyptians' wealth was incurred at the expense of others. As a result, it was stolen goods. God gave His people this command:

It shall be, when you go, that you shall not go empty-handed. But every woman shall ask of her neighbor, namely, of her who dwells

near her house, articles of silver, articles of gold, and clothing; and
you shall put them on your sons and on your daughters. So you shall
plunder the Egyptians. (Exodus 3.21–22)

Notice that the Scripture points out their current condition. They
were *"empty-handed,"* the result of 400 years of oppression. The people
had nothing. Oppression leads to poverty; ergo, when it came time to
leave, the children of Israel were to go to those who lived in close proximity, most often the very ones they had served, and ask for these resources
of gold, silver, and clothing.

The Egyptians knew what they had done to these people, and none of
them would have profited in the ways they had apart from exploiting this
large, free labor pool. This remuneration was more than due Israel. God
never hesitates in telling His people to ask for what is rightfully theirs.

Once they left Egypt, God began to describe in intimate detail what
life would be like in the new kingdom He was establishing, and one of
the things He repeatedly told His people was, "What happened to you,
you must never do to another person."

Do not mistreat an alien or oppress him, for you were aliens in Egypt.
Do not take advantage of a widow or orphan. If you do and they cry
out to me, I will certainly hear their cry....If you lend money to one
of my people among you who is needy, do not be like a moneylender;
charge him no interest. If you take your neighbors coat as a pledge, re-
turn it to him by sunset, because his cloak is the only covering he has
for his body. What else will he sleep in? When he cries out to me, I will
hear, for I am compassionate. (Exodus 22.21–27)

Built into God's righteous decrees that would govern His new nation
were provisions for vulnerable people. Oppression of others, exploiting
them for personal gain, and taking advantage of their desperation will
not be tolerated in God's new kingdom. Once God makes His decree
plain, what we read in the balance of the Old and even into the New
Testament is an absolute intolerance for laws or personal actions that oppress others.

One example of oppressive treatment of the poor in the above scripture is charging them interest on loans. In light of God's righteous decree, how do you think God feels about organizations today that not only charge interest to the poor, but charge at the highest rates allowable by law? How do you suppose God feels about those leaders in government charged with protecting the rights of the poor who are not only allowing this practice, but also are creating the very environment where this type of profiteering at the expense of poor is encouraged?

It reminds me of what Solomon said in Ecclesiastes.

If you see the poor oppressed in a district, and justice and rights denied, do not be surprised at such things; for one official is eyed by a higher one, and over them both are others higher still. (Ecclesiastes 5.8)

Corrupt laws are a form of oppression, according to God's Word. When laws are written in ways that deny the poor their rights or favor the rich at the expense of the poor, the Bible declares such laws as oppressive.

Woe to those who make unjust laws, to those who issue oppressive decrees, to deprive the poor of their rights and withhold justice from the oppressed of my people, making widows their prey and robbing the fatherless. (Isaiah 10.1–2)

In addition, holding onto essential items that are given as security on loans is also a face of oppression.

He does not oppress anyone, but returns what he took in pledge for a loan. (Ezekiel 18.7a)

Don't let anyone tell you otherwise; when officials take money so that they are biased toward the wealthy, God utterly condemns such practices.

For I know how many are your offenses and how great your sins. There are those who oppress the innocent and take bribes and deprive the poor of justice in the courts. (Amos 5.12)

To deprive a worker of his wage is another huge offense that provokes God's judgment.

> *So I will come to put you on trial. I will be quick to testify... against those who defraud laborers of their wages, who oppress the widows and the fatherless, and deprive the foreigners among you of justice, but do not fear me," says the LORD Almighty.* (Malachi 3.5)

This theme of oppression is woven throughout the entire Old Testament. They had 400 years to learn this lesson the hard way at the hands of the Egyptians. This lesson was burned into their collective psyche. God makes crystal clear that this type of treatment is absolutely intolerable.

In the book of Judges, we learn of men and women unlike judges today who wear robes, wield gavels, and preside over court cases. God's judges were a different breed entirely. The best way to describe them is champions of the oppressed. Once again, God is validating the value of the poor and vulnerable by raising up those whose job it is to defend and protect them.

Throughout Israel's history under its kings, some ruled righteously; others did not. When they failed to obey God's standards, a telltale sign of that failure was often oppression.

The major and minor prophets alike (those whom God raised up to speak truth to power) all have messages of correction to those who make use of oppressive power.

God literally had to raise up a group of men and women who would protect Israel from her own government. Such was the job of the prophets.

In addition, who can forget when Jesus enters the temple, literally to clean house? The very integrity of the house of God was at stake. What provoked Jesus' wrath was a corrupt system of exploitation of the poor. It's worth noting that the greatest anger Jesus ever expressed was directed toward those who were taking advantage of vulnerable people in the name of God. It was oppressive profiteering off the poor. Jesus, in keeping with God's righteous demands, drove the oppressors from the house of God.

Thus, the reason poverty is a justice issue. So much happens in our world that exploits and conspires against vulnerable people. Oppression either directly contributes to poverty, keeps people locked in poverty, or creates the condition in which poverty becomes a guaranteed eventuality.

In addition, there is still another face of oppression that I don't want to leave out. Oppression sometimes wears your face and my face, because according to God's Word, overconsumption is a form of oppression.

Think about Sodom and Gomorrah. When we hear the name Sodom, our minds immediately goes to sexual sin. For most who are reading this book, it's the kind of sin that we can honestly say we have never committed, but how often have you heard in church what Ezekiel, writing under the inspiration of the Holy Spirit, described as central to the judgment against Sodom?

Now this was the sin of your sister Sodom: She and her daughters were arrogant, overfed, and unconcerned; they did not help the poor and needy. (Ezekiel 16.49)

Arrogant, overfed, unconcerned, and not helping the poor – these are the major sins of the American Church. Most people in church have never even heard that verse mentioned when talking about the sin of Sodom. In fact, some of you are going to "fact check" me right now because you don't believe it. Go ahead. Please read the verse for yourself. I'm not suggesting that these were the only sins Sodom was judged for, but it is the very first thing that Ezekiel mentions.

It's also at the heart of what was wrong with the people. I think the real reason we avoid preaching the whole truth about Sodom's judgment is because it's much easier to get up on our high horse about homosexuality than it is to talk about the sin we see when we look into the mirror.

Being overfed and taking more than our fair share lie at the heart of our neglect of the poor because it becomes impossible to share with others when we have consumed it all for ourselves.

Do you remember how God made provisions for the poor in Israel's agricultural economy? Not only was there a special tithe that was received every third year for their care, but individuals also had a personal

X requirement placed on them every growing season. They were not to glean any of their fields completely. Instead, they were to leave the corners of their fields so that the poor could come and get food (Leviticus 19.9–10).

The message is clear, isn't it? To consume everything you grow is to deprive the poor. It's a form of oppression, for you are taking for yourself what rightfully belongs to others. God is saying that even the crop you grow by the sweat you produce is not all yours, because you wouldn't have grown it without God's help, and God expects you to share out of the abundance He creates.

Remember the story of the man with the bumper crop who decided he needed to build bigger barns (Luke 12)? God called the man a fool. In the story, the landowner spoke only of himself and to himself. Not once did he mention God or the good he might do for others, given his record-setting harvest. His only thought was hoarding, "How might I store this abundance and keep it all for myself?" The man was judged for his overconsumption.

Whenever I think that all I make is mine or all that I produce is mine, I commit the sin of oppression. Oppression is about justifying spending 100% of my resources on myself. The reason my selfish intent is oppressive is that resources which should exist to help people with legitimate needs are diminished because I have decided to keep my surplus, live beyond my means, or simply consume everything I earn. When I overconsume with no thought of others, I become numbered among the oppressors.

X Overconsumption, in a word, is the ancient sin of gluttony. I call it ancient, not because it isn't around anymore or that we have matured so much that we no longer commit this sin. I call it ancient because we don't talk about it anymore, nor do we preach about it. Gluttony is about tak-
X ing more than our fair share.

For the record, gluttony is not a sin because it makes you fat. Gluttony is a sin because it's eating at the expense of community. It's overconsumption of resources as if they belonged exclusively to us. Gluttony has never been limited to food. Whether it manifests itself in food, clothes, shoes, money, electronics, or lifestyles, overconsumption is the sin of gluttony.) When I hold tightly to my stuff while turning a deaf ear to the cries of people in need, I've committed the sin of gluttony. Overconsumption is gluttony, and gluttony is a form of oppression.

(When you truly understand that poverty is largely the byproduct of oppression, it means that charity will never be enough to solve the problem of poverty.) We will never simply be able to give more and, thereby, eradicate poverty. Think in terms of the parable you've likely heard of the man rescuing another man from drowning. One day, while walking along the river's edge, the man heard a cry for help coming from the river. Someone was drowning. The man immediately jumped into the water and pulled the drowning man to safety. No sooner did he get the victim to shore than he heard another cry of distress, followed by another, followed by another. (The moral: It's good to rescue those in distress, but it's even more important to go upstream and find the guy who's pushing all these people into the river and stop him.)

Money can address many of the ills and crises people face in the moment, but as long as there continues to be oppressive laws and practices, relief won't even begin to put a dent in poverty.

Oppression expresses itself in unfair laws and practices coupled with unthinking, over-consumptive behaviors. To dismantle systemic injustice requires a level of advocacy on behalf of the poor. Laws that unfairly target the poor have to be overturned. Exploitation of the poor by powers, whether they be governmental or personal, have to be brought into the light and challenged. People have to be taught that what they produce and what they own are not entirely theirs to do with as they please. Christ followers must be a voice for those who, because of their position in life, are never allowed a voice in places of power.

> *Speak up for the people who have no voice, for the rights of all the down-and-outers. Speak out for justice! Stand up for the poor and destitute!* (Proverbs 31.8)

> *Rescue the poor and helpless; deliver them from the grasp of evil people.* (Psalm 82.4)

The preceding verses speak to the issue of advocacy that goes beyond charity. Giving money is important, but giving our voice only happens when we understand how poverty goes beyond the tragic, unfortunate, and momentary. We give our voice when we understand that many of the world's poor are that way because they have been made that way through oppression. Someone has to tell the truth to government, to individuals, and to the Church. Someone has to speak up.

Advocacy is so aligned with the heart of God that when God summarized the life of King Josiah, he said, *He defended the cause of the poor and needy, and so all went well. Is that not what it means to know me?" declares the* LORD (Jeremiah 22.16).

To me, that God equates knowing Him with defending the cause of the poor and needy tells you how important advocacy really is. (The love we have for the poor must go beyond giving.) Just as the prophets were necessary to protect Israel from her own kings, we must speak up and speak truth to the powers that be, even if doing so means that we become numbered among the oppressed for speaking out (just like the prophets sometimes were), so be it.

To speak to the real issues that fuel cycles of poverty means that:

- The powers that be will consider us a threat and will label us with extreme terms in order to try to silence us.

- Speaking out against overconsumption will make us move against the grain of society and definitely will not win us any popularity contests.

- Some in our churches will walk away because they just don't want to hear the truth, and they can find plenty of other churches that won't address the poverty issue at all.

If, according to God Himself, the ones who truly know Him are the ones who are defending the cause of the poor and needy, then how many of us really know God?

Chapter 6

THEOLOGY
OF THE TABLE

MY SPIRITUAL DIRECTOR TELLS ME THAT NO ONE MAKES ANY real progress in the spiritual life unless and until they're willing to embrace their personal poverty. Her words are merely a reflection of Jesus' own words in Matthew 5.3, *"Blessed are the <u>poor in spirit</u>,..."*

As I said earlier, the poverty Jesus is talking about in Matthew is destitution or abject poverty. Basically, what Jesus is saying is, "The blessed life begins when we understand that we are begging poor in our spiritual life."

(To be poor in spirit means to recognize our true condition before ✗ God. In other words, we bring absolutely nothing to the Kingdom. We are <u>begging poor.</u>)

Objectively speaking, everyone is poor in spirit. Whether they sense it or not, whether they admit it or not, each one is bankrupt and helpless before God; however, when Jesus says, *"Blessed are the poor in spirit,"* He doesn't mean everybody. He means those who are in touch with that truth and live in that reality.

My personal belief is that a true understanding of being poor in spirit is the missing piece in missional theology. A missional theology that lacks an understanding of personal poverty is woefully inadequate. The reason this truth is so vitally important is unless we see ourselves as poor, we will never treat the poor as we should, because at a place deep within, we'll think of ourselves as either being "better" than the poor or "other than" the poor. Either approach is damned from the start.

The Bible teaches us that when we see the poor, we see ourselves. Their outer condition is a true reflection of our inner condition. Everything in the spiritual life begins with this baseline understanding of our own personal poverty.

When Jesus lays out for us the path of blessing in the beatitudes, he begins with a theology of poverty, *Blessed are the poor in spirit, for theirs is the kingdom of heaven…* " (Matthew 5.3). Our desperate poverty is what makes us cling to the Father. Being in touch with our poverty makes us less prone to judge, more compassionate with others, more humble in listening, and more patient with other "slow learners" like ourselves. No one makes any real progress in the spiritual life unless and until they are willing to embrace their own poverty.

If we are not in touch with our own poverty, we are not in touch with reality.

Sadly, because the Church loses connection with this primary truth in missional theology, many things are said and done in the name of helping the poor that bring harm and humiliation to them instead. Let me share with you the truths that brought this home to me.

 ✗   (In the Gospels, it was very important to Jesus to be "at a table" with people. The first miracle happened around a meal, at the wedding table in Cana of Galilee where he turned water into wine.)

Jesus also made a table in the wilderness when He fed the 5,000. This miracle is the only one recorded in all four Gospels, and the significance is that Jesus, just like his Father, is feeding His people manna in the desert.

The Gospels are permeated with Jesus welcoming the outcast, the tax collectors, and the prostitutes to a table. Eating with sinners was the norm for Jesus, not the exception.

Jesus spent His final hours at table with his disciples. We call it the Last Supper. He even left us, His Church, a permanent reminder of His sacrifice. It's called the Lord's Supper, Communion, or Eucharist. It's a holy meal celebrated by His followers at table. Even the last book in the Bible, the Revelation, reveals not just a wedding ceremony that consummates the ends of the ages, but also a table at the marriage supper of the Lamb.

(Now, why is the table so important? It's important because in Jesus' day, table customs were a mark of one's spirituality. To be at table with someone indicated your approval of them, explaining the reason Jesus' dinner companions got Him into so much trouble) Those He welcomed at table were the scandalous ones. It's also why His enemies leveled this accusation against Him, *He is a glutton and a drunkard, a friend of tax collectors and sinners* (Matthew 11.19). By His associations, Jesus made himself one of them. The company He kept at table was a reflection of those He approved of and identified with.

Obviously, Jesus saw the table very differently than His contemporaries. (To Him, the table was a place of fellowship and inclusion, a place of equality and acceptance.)

He would suffer because of His actions, so why did Jesus act in such a way? Because that was the way He loved us. Intentionally, Jesus was creating a place of inclusion and commonality at the table. By including those who His contemporaries scorned, He sent a message loud and clear: There are no second class citizens in the Kingdom of God, no "us" versus "them," no "poor" versus "rich." In Christ we are one. Consequently, I've always loved Eugene Peterson's paraphrase of 1 Corinthians 10…

> *"Because there is one loaf, our many-ness becomes one-ness... Christ doesn't become fragmented in us. Rather we become unified in Him."* (1 Corinthians 10.17, Message)

That's table theology and Jesus' vision for the Church. It's all about His people, the Body of Christ, becoming one. The table reminds us of our mission, our commonality, our equality, our love, and our acceptance of one another.

There was a time, however, very early in the history of the Church, that the theology of the table was compromised in a major way.

A few years ago, I was in San Diego at the National Pastors Conference, where I sat in on a talk about power in the context of the global Church. Dr. Athena Gorospe, a professor who teaches at Asian Theological Seminary, was one of the presenters. I have never heard anyone speak with greater power, humility, and conviction than Dr. Gorospe.

I am deeply in her debt and humbled by her willingness to teach me what I'm about to share with you.

There were only about a dozen of us in the room that day when Dr. Gorospe shared a story about the church in Corinth. As you may recall, Corinth was a fairly large congregation. Most of the members were very poor, but a few who were wealthy and influential people were also a part of the church, which is why Paul wrote in 1 Corinthians 1.26, *Brothers, think of what you were when you were called. Not many of you were wise by human standards; not many were influential; not many were of noble birth.*

Paul was not saying there weren't any wealthy people at Corinth, just not many. The wealthy members opened their homes as a place for the church to gather. Out of their own resources, they would host itinerate preachers. In addition, they were the ones who provided food and drink for the Lord's Supper.

Soon a practice developed in the Corinthian church that turned their giving into something that actually humiliated the poor. This practice was known as the patronage system. To get what was really going on in Corinth, you have to understand the dynamic of the patron-client relationship.

A patron-client relationship exists when a patron who has money and other resources gives the client what he or she needs or what he or she wants. You say, "What's wrong with that?"

Dr. Gorospe did a masterful job of explaining the dynamic behind a patron-client relationship. What it came down to was a fundamental inequality in power. In the patron-client relationship, patrons and clients are not equal in terms of power. The patrons are not needy or dependent. They really hold all the power, because they have all the money. The clients, on the other hand, are the truly needy ones; they are dependent. They typically don't have many resources and are not in positions of leadership and decision-making.

This inequity in power manifested itself in Corinth around the Lord's Table, the very place where there was to be total equality and acceptance in the Body of Christ.

Imagine this scenario. The church gathered, as it always did, in the home of the wealthy members. There was a meal that was shared in association with the Lord's Supper. The gathering place and the meal were provided by the hosts, the wealthy patrons.

In these private homes, the dining room and table could only accommodate so many people. Of course, being the wealthy patron's home and his food, he would invite his favorites—usually those with the same status and wealth—to eat and drink with him at table. Everybody else would have to eat either in one of the other rooms or outside. Those at table were served better food and wine, and more of it, while the others outside got less, both in terms of quality and quantity.

This practice made the poor feel excluded and humiliated. Listen to Paul sum up the situation in I Corinthians 11.20–22…

> When you come together, it is not the Lord's Supper you eat, for as you eat, each of you goes ahead without waiting for anybody else. One remains hungry, another gets drunk. Don't you have homes to eat and drink in? Or do you despise the church of God and humiliate those who have nothing? What shall I say to you? Shall I praise you for this? Certainly not!

According to Paul, when the church came together for the Lord's Supper, the poor were not getting enough to eat and drink, while others had so much they were gluttonous and drunk. It's quite an amazing contrast between overconsumption and deprivation going on side by side in the church around the Lord's table. Disparity between the haves and the have-nots was amplified in a meal intended to show equality.

Now, try to put yourself in the shoes of one of the poor saints in Corinth. If you were poor and you watched while the wealthy ate and drank more than their fill, yet the morsels you were given didn't even stop your stomach from growling, how would you feel? You couldn't really complain about unfairness, could you? How do you complain about not getting enough when you are not the one providing the meal in the first place?

So, at the table where everyone should experience equality and acceptance, you are made acutely aware of the fact that you have nothing, and because you have nothing, you don't feel that you have a right to speak up. There would be plenty to go around if the rich weren't overconsuming, but who are you to point out their behavior? Understandably, the feeling that you feel most strongly is an overwhelming sense of humiliation. At the place where everyone should feel love, acceptance, and equality with one another, you're reminded that you're not like the rest: You are a beggar.

In our culture, we have a saying, "Beggars can't be choosers." In other words, we believe the poor have no rights to ask for what they need. In our minds, a beggar's only right is to accept without complaint whatever we choose to give out of the good graces of our hearts. The privilege of having a choice is stripped from the poor, while at the same time, our status as benefactor is well established. It is this fundamental inequity of power that lies at the heart of the patron-client relationship, and that's what was going on in Corinth.

Given the same situation, many would say, "What right does the poor have to complain about being treated unfairly? They're not providing the meal. It's a gift. Beggars can't be choosers."

While that thinking may characterize our culture, make no mistake about it, God absolutely rejects it. Paul said this type of giving *humiliates those who have nothing* (1 Corinthians 11.22). To give in such a way as to make the poor even more conscious of their poverty is reprehensible. God considers the practice a degrading, disgusting insult to the poor.

When the only choices we permit the poor are take it or leave it, like it or lump it, submit or shut up, we are playing the power game and creating winners and losers. Charitable intentions cease the moment we begin to use wealth as power so that the poor are humiliated and made to feel conscious of their lack.

Paul calls out this behavior and then makes this statement in 1 Corinthians 11.29 ... *For he that eats and drinks in an unworthy manner, eats and drinks damnation to their soul,* (WHY?) *because they are not discerning the Body of Christ.*

Now, in my Baptist upbringing, I was always taught that that verse meant if you don't understand that the bread and cup represent Jesus, then you're in danger of the judgment, but that's not what this verse means at all. Given the backdrop of what is actually going on in Corinth, that interpretation seems to be a wild departure from everything Paul has said up to this point.

Paul is indicting the patron-client relationship. What he's saying is, "If you participate in the Lord's Supper in this way, bringing humiliation on the poor by making them conscious of their poverty, you are eating and drinking your own damnation." When Paul says that the patrons have failed to discern the Body of Christ, he's not referring to the elements of communion. Instead, he is talking about their poor brothers and sisters in Christ. God's people are the Body of Christ. If I eat and drink in such a manner so as not to discern the Body of Christ in its fullness seated around the table, I am consuming my own judgment.

In truth, Paul's message is really the same message that Jesus gave us in Matthew 25. In the only place in Scripture where Jesus speaks extensively of the final judgment, He makes clear that judgment falls on those who fail to discern that needy and vulnerable people represent Him: To fail to care for them is to fail to care for Christ. Jesus asked, "I was hungry, did you feed me? I was thirsty, did you give me something to drink?" If not, then Jesus will respond, *"Depart from Me, you who are cursed"* (Matthew 25.41). In God's Word, judgment falls on those who treat Christ (as He is represented in vulnerable people) with disdain.

In essence, Paul warns if we continue this dishonorable practice around the Lord's table, not discerning that the poor are members of Christ's body, we're actually eating and drinking our own judgment. In other words, it's not okay to treat Jesus in this way! Humiliating the poor by making them more conscious of their poverty is failing to discern the Body of Christ. Treating the poor as anything less than our equal is to invite the judgment of God.

Once Dr. Gorospe finished explaining this dynamic as it played itself out in the Corinthian congregation, I had that sickening feeling once again that I had been doing ministry and mission all wrong. Her teaching convicted me to the core. No matter how well intentioned I had been, I was numbered among the patrons.

When we engaged in mission, we had replicated the patron-client relationship in 21st century shoe leather. We meant well. We sincerely desired to help people, but nothing can change the fact that we had done it wrong.

How many of our churches today are more like Corinth than we care to admit?

χ (It seems to be a default in our culture to think that because we have money, that gives us rights as opposed to responsibilities.) We think we should determine what we want to do. We think that the one who has the resources has the rights to tell others what to do and who gets what. And the poor? Well, they should just be happy that we're helping them at all.

We may be sincere in our desire to help, but we are sincerely wrong in our approach. We come having already decided what we want to do. Let's be honest, there is no real partnership or sense of equality when one party sets the agenda, makes all the decisions, and gives the other party only room to consent. Having a preconceived agenda is not a partnership. It's exploitation.

God's Church must get back to the table where in humility we can say, "Maybe we don't know what's best. Maybe God is already doing something in Africa, in Asia, in Central America, or in our own community. Maybe if we considered our poor brothers and sisters every bit our equal, we would stop force feeding them our solutions and start listening to their solutions." It's then, and only then, that we can begin resourcing what God is already doing.

Bruce Wilkinson is the author of the best-selling book *The Prayer of Jabez*. He made a big splash a number of years ago when he announced his ambitious plan to help children suffering from AIDS in Swaziland, but the grand scheme didn't work out for Wilkinson like he thought it would.

The Wall Street Journal did a page one feature on what went wrong, "In 2002, Bruce Wilkinson, a Georgia preacher whose self-help prayer book had made him a rich man, heard God's call, moved to Africa and announced his intention to save one million children left orphaned by the AIDS epidemic. In October [2005], Wilkinson resigned in a huff from the African charity he founded. He abandoned his plan to house 10,000 children in a facility that was to be an orphanage, bed-and-breakfast, game reserve, Bible college, industrial park, and Disneyesque tourist destination in the tiny kingdom of Swaziland. What happened in between is a story of grand hopes and inexperience, divine inspiration and human foibles. His departure left critics convinced he was just another in a long parade of outsiders who have come to Africa making big promises and quit the continent when local people didn't bend to their will." [1]

I don't relate this story to condemn Wilkinson but to point out a problem that pervades the American Church. It's the patron-client relationship. We assume that because we have the resources, we get to make all the decisions about how to best use the money, and the poor should just accept the things we want to do.

Such tactics are common in American churches. We travel overseas, witness firsthand a level of deprivation unlike anything we've ever seen before, and then return home to make our plans and execute our decisions about what we want to do. We pull our chairs up to the table and divvy out the morsels, expecting the poor to be grateful. We didn't really involve them in the discussion or the decision-making, are not really working alongside them as equals, and don't really care if what we want to do fits with their priorities, because we don't see them as we see ourselves…they're just poor. We're the benefactors. We're the wealthy patrons.

Today, much of what the Church calls "giving to the poor" is actually just humiliating the poor, because it keeps us in the driver's seat and reinforces the thinking of the world that exalts money and power at the expense of the poor.

In the prior chapter, we talked about oppression as a root cause of most poverty. There is another form of oppression that I intentionally left out because you needed a larger context in order to understand it.

Even giving can be a form of oppression when it's done in this way. The reason it's oppressive is because it reinforces a distorted view of the poor as beneath us. Oppression, by nature, keeps people down. When giving reinforces my position as benefactor and strips choice away from those I presume to help, I become numbered among the oppressors.

(A Bishop from Uganda, Dr. David Zac Niringiye, once said, "Africa's crisis is not poverty; it is not AIDS. Africa's crisis is confidence.)What decades of colonialism and missionary enterprise eroded among us is confidence. So a 'national leader' from the United States comes—he may have a good-sized congregation, but he knows nothing about Africa!—and we defer to him. We don't even tell him everything we are thinking, out of respect. We Africans must constantly repent of that sense of inferiority." [2]

I think Bishop Zac is right. Africa has a confidence problem. So what happens when well-meaning Americans show up and dig wells for them and build schools for them? The same thing that happens when your kids have projects at school that they need your help with and you take it from them. You take it from their hands and say, "Let me do it. You're messing it up." What have your kids learned? You could say they haven't learned anything, but that's not true. What they've learned is that they can't do it themselves.

We've reinforced whatever inferiority they may be feeling by making them even more conscious of their inadequacy. Thus my insistence that there is a difference between helping and creating dependencies. There is a difference between resourcing and disempowering. There is a difference between investing and taking over.)

As a church, we want to help. We want to help resource the poor and make a difference in their lives, but we don't want to create dependencies. We don't want to send a message that they're incapable of helping themselves, and we most certainly do not want to yank projects out of their hands and say, "Let me do it. You're just messing it up."

If we do any of those things, then we've actually done something far worse to them than their poverty has ever done. We've actually added to their poverty. People who merely lacked resources now feel impoverished in their minds and abilities.

These attitudes have been around a long time. Think about it. Paul is writing about this stuff in the first century, yet this patron-client mentality is still alive and well today and defines far too much of what we do in terms of mission.

But there is hope, and it's found at table. The meal that Jesus left for us has a life-changing spiritual truth at its core. On that table is a loaf of bread. Jesus tells us when we come together to commemorate the Lord's Supper, the bread is blessed and then broken. Broken bread lies at the heart of this holy meal as a reminder that the table is the fellowship of the broken.

We must never lose sight of this truth. We must never lose touch with our own brokenness, our own personal poverty. As I've already said, no one makes any real progress in the spiritual life unless or until he embraces his own brokenness.

(The missing piece in missional theology is the theology of personal ✗ brokenness.)We must never forget that we are as broken as any other soul around the table. It's only when we remember this that we will then treat our brothers and sisters as equals. We won't think of wealth as a right but a responsibility. Most of all, when we give, the poor will not be humiliated. Instead, they will be honored, held in high esteem for their contribution, and loved like the family they are, and everyone will have enough.

Chapter 7

THE GOSPEL OF JUBILEE

I HOPE YOU'RE BEGINNING TO SEE why I said that our apology itself was rather anticlimactic. Taking responsibility for how we got it wrong was relatively easy compared to what God had to do to open our blinded eyes and strip away our excuses. In light of everything God had shown us, the apology was just the next right thing to do.

The connection between economics and the Gospel would be next on God's agenda for us. Jesuit theologian Fr. John Haughey offers the best commentary on today's church, "We read the Gospel as if we had no money, and we spend our money as if we know nothing of the Gospel." [1]

Talking about money in church has always been challenging, but getting people to understand the economic implications of the Gospel is even more difficult.

As Christians, our theology is supposed to define our economic priorities. Sadly, our stewardship classes are woefully lacking when it comes to these bigger economic realities. Oh, sure, we do an excellent job on the part about debt, saving, investing, and giving to the church. Those topics all serve our personal needs, but the big-picture stuff, the more communal aspects of our financial planning and behavior, is left unaddressed.

It's like Ron Sider once said, "God is on the side of the poor and the oppressed. Tragically, evangelical theology has largely ignored this doctrine, and thus our theology has been unbiblical — indeed, even heretical — on this important point." [2]

Biblically, when it comes to issues of money and economy, the bible repeatedly returns a number of givens:

- God created a world of abundance, where there is more than enough for everyone as long as people practice restraint and live within their limits.

- Disparity between the haves and the have-nots is not natural or normal. Disparity is the result of sin.

- God calls on us to share our resources because they are His resources. Hoarding and overconsumption are always wrong.

Of course, our world knows nothing of God's value system. It exists in defiance of God's laws and expectations. In our world, inequality is rampant. People adamantly refuse to live within limits. Instead, they are focused almost exclusively on themselves and their own needs, and taking more than one's fair share is seen as the reward of our diligent work, but what is true of the world system is not to be the thing that defines the people of God.

God tells us to resist the system. In the words of Paul, *Don't let the world around you squeeze you into its mold...* (Romans 12.2 – Phillips). Instead, God's people must be transformed, changed in order to live in new ways, God's ways.

All of the following - disparity, hoarding, entitlement, and inequality - are examples of injustice. They are not right and never were they to be tolerated among God's people. What we see when we look at the Old Testament is a God who is intentional about ridding His people of these vices. Of course, there are numerous ways where God made provision for the needs of vulnerable people within Israel's economy. These statutes were intended to keep human depravity in check and allow all of God's people to flourish.

One statute that clearly establishes poverty as a justice issue is Jubilee. In agrarian societies, such as ancient Israel or even parts of the developing world today, poverty often enters through a crisis such as illness or drought, which requires a family to go into debt. As the debt deepens, people are forced into selling their assets in order to satisfy the debt. Typically, the one asset they have is their land. People without property have only their labor left to sell, and they become slaves, or virtual slaves, working for whatever they can get, often accepting an unlivable wage. Thus the reason the Bible says, *The rich rule over the poor, and the borrower is slave to the lender* (Proverbs 22.7).

In ancient times, there were no banks, so landowners often acted as creditors. Imagine you are a father, the head of the household, and fell ill incurring medical costs. The illness leaves you unable to work the family farm and you fear your crops might utterly fail. Yet your family must eat. What do you do when you don't have the wherewithal to provide for yourself because of an illness beyond your control? In the absence of any social safety nets or extended family to care for you, your only choice is to liquidate the only assets you have. Your land, your farm, your independence have to be sacrificed in order to provide for your family.

A wealthy landowner might acquire your property, even allow you to remain on the land, but now you are working for him, and the crops you produce are no longer your own. The money you received for your land satisfies your creditors but won't last forever. You are now servant to another. You can no longer merely work harder to turn your situation around. Even a bumper crop won't significantly alter your life or future, because that blessing is now given to another. A setback like this in life can be unrecoverable.

God, in His wisdom, understands how poverty overtakes families, so He established a pattern, a way of righting the course. It was nothing short of a complete reset of the system. It was called Jubilee. It was to happen every 50th year. When you think about average life expectancies, what that means is once in your lifetime, you would get to experience Jubilee.

When you read Leviticus 25 where God defines Jubilee, you see the scope of God's provisions for the 50th year:

- Whatever debt you had accrued would be completely wiped out and forgiven.

- All land that had been forfeited would be returned to its original owners.

- All slaves would be freed. (Remember, slavery was, for the most part, the result of debt.)

Every provision in the law of Jubilee is tied to poverty and resetting the system to give those locked in a state of permadebt a new beginning. In the 50th year, you were given an opportunity to get back on your feet again. Not just freedom from servitude but a restoration of assets once lost.

In Jubilee, God was saying, "It is not good for the gap between the haves and the have-nots to grow perpetually. Something in the system itself must be in place to stop it, because human depravity will always game the system to personal advantage, and human depravity will take advantage of another's desperation in order to gain the upper hand."

God, who knows this propensity in the human heart, made sure that even though depravity might prevail in the moment, it wouldn't prevail for a lifetime. God would right the record books, balance the scales of justice, and restore what was lost. It's really quite amazing what God envisioned in the Jubilee.

There's just one problem with Jubilee, and it's not God's righteous intentions or His provisions. It really comes back to human depravity. It won. Human depravity won out over God's laws, because even though God commanded Jubilee, as Warren Wiersbe pointed out, "There's no evidence in Scripture that the nation of Israel ever celebrated the year of Jubilee." [3]

In other words, the rich and the powerful held onto their gains, the poor stayed locked in their debtors' prisons, and the heart of God was broken. How could that be? How could the people of God so flagrantly disregard God's desires? That's a really important question. This disregard is not just about what happened in ancient Israel; it's also about us. Why do we do it? Why do we, in the words of John Haughey, "read the Gospels as if we had no money, and we spend our money as if we know nothing of the Gospel"?

I'm not going to offer an answer. Let it ruminate in your spirit for a while as I take you further into this teaching.

Listen to the Old Testament prophets in light of this reality. You'll be surprised at how much you missed, skipped over, and were blind to that which indicts Israel for the inequity that she allowed to grow between rich and poor. Messages we hear repeated through the prophets are warnings of overconsumption, exploitation of the poor, and the cry of the widow and orphan in their distress. One thing is certain: The cry of injustice reaches the heart of God and prompts His intervention.

Although the people of God refused to listen to God, He didn't give up on this idea of Jubilee. Isaiah spoke of a time that was coming when the "Anointed One" would arrive and proclaim Jubilee.

> *The Spirit of the Sovereign Lord is on me, because the Lord has anointed me to preach good news to the poor. He has sent me to bind up the brokenhearted, to proclaim freedom for the captives and release from darkness for the prisoners...* (Isaiah 61.1)

Isaiah is talking about the Jubilee and is clearly tying the concept to the Messianic hope. Because the powers that be refused to enact God's Jubilee provisions, Israel came to understand that it would take someone greater than their kings to make it happen. It would take a truly righteous King, the rightful ruler over God's people, to make good on God's promise of Jubilee. This became their hope and their prayer: When the Messiah comes, He will usher in Jubilee.

For this purpose, Luke 4 is so compelling. Jesus is home in Nazareth. It's the Sabbath day, and He goes to the local synagogue. He's going to teach the people, so He opens the scroll to Isaiah and reads, *The Spirit of the Lord is on me, because he has anointed me to preach good news to the poor. He has sent me to proclaim freedom for the prisoners and recovery of sight for the blind, to release the oppressed, to proclaim the year of the Lord's favor. Then he rolled up the scroll, gave it back to the attendant and sat down. The eyes of everyone in the synagogue were fastened on him, and he began by saying to them, "Today this scripture is fulfilled in your hearing."* (Luke 4.18–21)

Jesus has just declared Jubilee. Isaiah had foretold that the "Anointed One" is the one who would accomplish such. Isaiah's words were the mark of the Messiah's credentials, so when Jesus said, *"Today this scrip-ture is fulfilled in your hearing,"* people clearly understood the implica-tions. Jesus was declaring Himself to be the Messiah.

The law had been powerless to bring about the Jubilee, Israel's kings were too corrupt to enact it, and her priests also seemed to lack the will to make it so. But what ancient Israel refused to do, Jesus would now do.

Jesus is describing the Kingdom of God and a new way of being in the world. Love would now make happen what could not and would not happen through force of law. He's not proclaiming a single year of the Lord's favor but a Jubilee for all time. He's declaring the age of the Lord's favor.

A number of years ago Bono (founding member of the band U2) was asked to speak at the National Prayer Breakfast in Washington D.C. His topic was Jubilee. Bono was, for all intents and purposes, an anointed prophet, for he spoke these words to pastors and national leaders…

> "What he (Jesus) was really talking about was an era of grace—and we're still in it. Look, whatever thoughts you have about God, who He is or if He exists, most will agree that if there is a God, He has a special place for the poor. In fact, the poor are where God lives.
>
> "Check Judaism. Check Islam. Check pretty much anyone.
>
> "I mean, God may well be with us in our mansions on the hill… I hope so. He may well be with us as in all manner of controversial stuff… maybe, maybe not… But the one thing we can all agree, all faiths and ideologies, is that God is with the vulnerable and poor…
>
> "God is in the slums, in the cardboard boxes where the poor play house… God is in the silence of a mother who has infected her child with a virus that will end both their lives… God is in the cries heard under the rubble of war… God is in the debris of wasted opportunity and lives, and God is with us if we are with them." [4]

Bono's words echo what Jesus was saying, "It's Jubilee, and my people will now make it happen."

If you look at Jesus' teaching in light of this reality, especially the Gospel of Luke where this teaching occurs, you'll see the spirit of Jubilee in practically everything He says. Here are just a couple of examples.

Jesus taught his disciples to pray, *forgive us our debts, as we also have forgiven our debtors* (Matthew 6.12). In other words, "When you see your brother is trapped in debt, just forgive it and give him an opportunity to begin again." In God's economy, we perpetually live in the spirit of Jubilee. It goes beyond a once-in-a-lifetime do-over. People are valued over things. Injustice is recognized in the immediate and remedied. People are set free to live and love as God intended.

When you give a banquet, you are not just to invite your rich friends or those with the ability to repay the kindness. You are to invite the poor, the crippled, the blind, and the lame. That's Jubilee! It's about creating opportunity where none existed before and breaking down the divisions between rich and poor (Luke 14.12–14).

When Jesus describes the rich man as one who builds bigger and bigger barns, whose life is defined by the accumulation of stuff, God said the man was a fool. Why? Because the man was living in the spirit of this age. His overconsumption defined him. His ignorance of his neighbor indicted him, and Jesus was warning His followers of the dangers of living like that man (Luke 12.13–21).

The story of the rich man and Lazarus (Luke 16.19–31) and the story of Zacchaeus (Luke 19.1–10), these are all stories meant to teach us how Christ is ushering in the Kingdom of God and that with it come new spiritual realities and economic implications.

Jesus entered into oneness with the poor, the oppressed, and the captives in order to set them free. Of course, we understand that there is a spiritual poverty and captivity even greater than the material, and I don't want to diminish that for one minute, but I also don't want to do as I've done in the past, "spiritualize" these passages, gut them of their clear economic implications, and congratulate myself that I understand and practice all these things.

One simply cannot reconcile a "spiritualized" reading of these passages with the reality of Jesus' choice of a life of poverty, the example of the early Church, and the chord that runs from cover to cover in the Bible about God's bias toward the poor.

I stand unapologetically with Jesus. He is teaching new ways of living and being in the world. Following in His steps is about living in the spirit of Jubilee. The proclamation of the Gospel begins with the announcement of Jubilee.

Back to my question: Why do we fail to practice the ways of Jubilee? Why do we hear the plain teaching of Scripture and immediately in our mind try to invalidate it, create exceptions for ourselves, or gut it of its hard-hitting implications? Do we think ourselves immune to the seductive power of money and power? Have we somehow convinced ourselves that God's idea of Jubilee was just out of an Old Testament concern and that, under grace, we are now freed to live selfishly? Consider the words of the apostle James...

> Now listen, you rich people, weep and wail because of the misery that is coming on you. Your wealth has rotted, and moths have eaten your clothes. Your gold and silver are corroded. Their corrosion will testify against you and eat your flesh like fire. You have hoarded wealth in the last days. Look! The wages you failed to pay the workers who mowed your fields are crying out against you. The cries of the harvesters have reached the ears of the Lord Almighty. You have lived on earth in luxury and self-indulgence. You have fattened yourselves in the day of slaughter. (James 5.1–5)

James is writing to first-century believers. He indicts them for trusting in their short-lived wealth, taking advantage of others, and living self-indulgently. God obviously expects much more of us than we require of ourselves. ("To whom much is given," said Jesus, "much will be required" (Luke 12.48).) We simply must stop thinking of wealth as our right and begin to see it as God does, a tremendous responsibility.

Through years of practical engagement in global relief efforts, World Vision has discovered if the elderly and the very young are not thriving in a community, then it's only a matter of time before the entire community will be in crisis. In a similar way, God too looks to the vulnerable ones among us as a barometer of the condition of the community.

There is a direct correlation between the POVERTY index and the SIN index. When poverty is on the rise, sin is too.

Why is that? It's because of the nature of sin itself. Isaiah once declared, ("We all, like sheep, have gone astray, each of us has turned to our own way..." (Isaiah 53.6). I've never found a better definition for sin. Sin is fundamentally about wanting my own way. In other words, I want what I want more than I want what God wants) That stubborn selfishness lies at the heart of every sinful choice. No wonder God looks to the poor to determine how sinful a nation is. The more it neglects its obligations to those without, the further it has moved from the heart of God. The more selfish it is, the more sinful it is. Nothing speaks as loudly about the condition of the human heart more than neglect of the poor.

Sadly, we have a political narrative in this country regarding poverty that is out of sync with God's Word. It's politically expedient to blame the poor for their poverty, but in the 1600-year history that the Bible spans, God lays the greater part of blame on the selfishness of others. Systemic injustice is the root cause of most of this world's poverty.

In the Bible, when the poor cry out, God hears. Again and again the poor cry out and each time God listens and responds. Without fail, judgment falls on the oppressor. Of course, this judgment would make no sense at all if poverty could be attributed mostly to the behavior of the poor. Why would God be judging others for something that the poor inflicted upon themselves? Judgment, however, doesn't fall on the poor; it falls on those who oppress them.

Both the Old and New Testament alike constantly associate God's judgment with our treatment of the poor. When Solomon speaks of righteousness exalting a nation, it's not by accident that prior to that he says, ("Whoever oppresses the poor shows contempt for their Maker, but whoever is kind to the needy honors God." (Proverbs 14.31))

When Jesus declared Jubilee, He was announcing a radical new shift in the way His people were to live in the world. God has laid the ax to the roots of how poverty is perpetuated. He is going after the sin issue that has a stranglehold on our hearts. His desire is to free us from self-centered thinking and living in order that we might live constantly in the spirit of Jubilee. The wrongs will not accumulate and perpetuate as they have before. Hearts that are set free from selfishness (sin) will relate in entirely new ways to their neighbors.

Do we show evidence of this change? If Jubilee is about setting captives free, forgiving debts, establishing justice, and giving people who are trapped an opportunity to begin afresh with the resources they need, then am I really living Jubilee?

Once again, Jubilee is a reminder that poverty goes beyond a lack of stuff. There is great injustice in the world - and often times, even among God's people - injustice that keeps people trapped in poverty without hope of remedy. In the spirit of Jubilee, the Church is called to enter the darkest of circumstances with hope for a new beginning. Our message is one of freedom for the captive, restoration for our losses, and forgiveness for the burden of debt.

Truly, this is what it means to be a child of God. All of our circumstances have happened for us in a spiritual sense, but please don't diminish the significance of Jubilee by spiritualizing its application. God is not okay with a world that criminalizes poverty, values money over people, allows greed to wreck our economy, and destroys the lives of vulnerable people. This world is not as it should be. Sin has moved beyond the individual and has infected everything people have touched. The whole world is crying out for redemption.

Jubilee is the vision of a preferred future condition. It's God's beachhead in a world that is hostile to His value system. Whether the world practices it or not, we will, and we will ever be God's prophetic voice to any and all powers that exist in the world that this is the heart of God. ✗ (The love of Christ has set us free to believe and practice Jubilee.)

Chapter 8

THE BOOK OF ACTS HAS A PRIMER

THE BOOK OF ACTS IS OFTEN CELEBRATED IN MANY CHURCHES as their guiding compass. Many speak of getting back to their roots, to the Church as it was meant to be in Acts. It's hard not to love the Book of Acts. Its history chronicling the explosive growth of the first-century church is truly awe-inspiring, but the key to unlocking the greatness of Luke's second work is found in his first work, the Gospel of Luke.

It's my belief that the Gospel of Luke represents the THEOLOGY of the early Christian movement, and the Book of Acts represents the PRACTICE. Luke lays the foundation for understanding the Kingdom of God as an expression of Jubilee. Then Acts dramatizes what Jubilee looks like as it's lived out in the life of the church. No church can ever be an Acts church apart from understanding the theological imperative of the Gospel of Luke.

The opening salvo in the Gospel of Luke is the voice of a lone woman. It's a prayer, written in the form of a song by a 15-year-old girl. Some consider it the most influential song ever written. Traditionally, it's been called "the Magnificat" (from the first word of the Latin version), which means, "My soul magnifies the Lord."

It was written by Mary, the mother of Jesus. It sounds a lot like the Psalms. There are also strong similarities with the song of Hannah in 1 Samuel 2. Mary lays the groundwork for the Gospel of Luke in chapter 1, beginning with verse 45 ...

And Mary said: "My soul glorifies the Lord, and my spirit rejoices in God my Savior, for He has been mindful of the humble state of His servant.

From now on all generations will call me blessed, for the Mighty One has done great things for me—holy is His name. His mercy extends to those who fear Him, from generation to generation. He has performed mighty deeds with His arm; He has scattered those who are proud in their inmost thoughts. He has brought down rulers from their thrones but has lifted up the humble. He has filled the hungry with good things, but has sent the rich away empty. He has helped His servant Israel, remembering to be merciful to Abraham and His descendants forever, just as he promised our ancestors." (Luke 1.45–55)

Mary's discourse is radical stuff. Mary envisions a new Kingdom unlike anything that has gone before. The great injustices of society will be righted. Arrogant rulers will be overthrown, and the humble exalted in their stead. Mary sees hungry bellies being filled, and those who preyed on the vulnerable, the rich, experiencing a reversal of fortune.

This vision Mary sees is consistent with the Jewish Messianic hope that the Anointed One would set things right in a world full of injustice. (She is singing a song of hope that her Son will continue to sing. Her expectation is God's expectation.)

Have you ever wondered why this broad indictment of the rich in Mary's song? Aren't there good rich people? Aren't there examples of godly wealthy people in the Bible? Yes, of course there are, but the rich are given abundant caution from God to not put their trust in wealth, and instead be rich where it counts; that is, to have treasure in heaven. (We lay up treasure in heaven through generosity and willingness to share.)

 Command those who are rich in this present world not to be arrogant nor to put their hope in wealth, which is so uncertain, but to put their hope in God, who richly provides us with everything for our enjoyment. Command them to do good, to be rich in good deeds, and to be generous and willing to share. In this way they will lay up treasure for themselves as a firm foundation for the coming age, so that they may take hold of the life that is truly life. (1 Timothy 6.17–19)

So back to the original question: Why such a broad indictment on the rich? Because as a general rule, what we see in the Bible is the rich getting richer at the expense of others, most often coming in the form of over-gathering of resources so that there is less to go around, or refusing to share the abundance God has provided. In other words, greed and selfishness lie at the heart of this indictment.

The radical nature of what Mary said has not been lost on Bible scholars. Bruce Larson relates, "William Temple, Archbishop of Canterbury, warned his missionaries to India never to read the Magnificat in public. Christians were already suspect in that country, and they were cautioned against reading verses so inflammatory. Jesus, the ultimate revolutionary, completely reverses all human values." [1]

Dr. E. Stanley Jones said about Mary's song, "Here, then, was a new Kingdom which was to precipitate a general revolution in scattering the proud, a political revolution in putting down princes from their thrones, a social revolution in exalting them of low degree, and an economic revolution in filling the hungry with good things and turning the rich empty away." [2]

The English theologian William Barclay wrote, "There is loveliness in the Magnificat, but in that loveliness there is dynamite. Christianity begets a revolution in each man and revolution in the world." [3]

The Protestant Reformer Martin Luther wrote the following about the Magnificat. "He comforts those who must suffer wrong... (and) those who must suffer injury and evil. And as much as He comforts the latter, so much does He terrify the former." [4] In other words, God comforts the lowly and terrifies the rich.

There's no getting around the fact that this message is radical, even downright revolutionary. Luke puts it first because it sets the tone for his book. It adjusts our point of view to see Christ's mission through God's eyes. It radically reprioritizes our value system to reflect God's perspective. What Mary says in the Magnificat is integral to everything Luke is about to lay out. Mary's themes are Luke's themes. The chord she strikes is the same one her Son will continue.

The poor permeate the Gospel of Luke. In fact, the Gospel of Luke has been called "The Gospel of the Poor." You see this in simple things like the birth of Christ. The ones who came to the manger and praised the Lord are the poor and humble shepherds. Only Luke tells us of Jesus' humble birth circumstances, the entourage that surrounded Him, and the stark nature of the stable.

As we move deeper into Luke's narrative, we're introduced to John the Baptist and his message of repentance. Luke specifically tells us what John said repentance should look like. *Whoever has two coats must share with anyone who has none; and whoever has food must do likewise* (Luke 3.11). In other words, a repentant heart, a heart that has fundamentally changed, is a heart that shares with others.

Shortly after this, in Luke 4, we have Jesus' first sermon in Nazareth. And that sermon is the one I've already told you about: It's the announcement of Jubilee. Jubilee is the perfect complement to Mary's song. You could say that Jubilee is the "second stanza" to Mary's song. Jesus was singing His Mom's song.

In Luke 7, John the Baptist has been arrested and looks like he's going to be killed. In his final moments, he begins to struggle with doubt, so he sends his messengers to ask if Jesus is really the Messiah. Do you remember what Jesus said in response? *Tell John, "The blind see. The lame walk. The lepers are cleansed. The deaf hear. The poor have good news preached to them."* (Luke 7.22) Jesus' answer to John is Jubilee. He's saying, "I am the Jubilee. I am the good news to the poor. This is Who Messiah is. This is what Messiah does."

Luke is writing the Gospel for the poor. Dr. Walter Pilgrim wrote a book about Luke called, *Good News for the Poor*. In his book, Pilgrim says that modern Christians spiritualize the verses in Luke in order to try to water them down and minimize them. He wrote, "The hungry become those hungering for God's Word, or the poor become the poor in spirit, or the sick and imprisoned become those suffering from sin ... (but) we need to keep our minds open to the full meaning of salvation in the Scriptures, which never divide the material from the spiritual, the soul from the body." [5]

Pilgrim's assertion is so true. So why do we divide the material from the spiritual? We do it because Luke's words make us uncomfortable. It speaks to the way we really live. Accepting Jesus' teaching at face value makes us look in the mirror and see our own selfishness.

Almost all of the parables Luke recorded in some way reinforce the message of Jubilee;

- the creditor and two debtors (Luke 7.40–50)

- the good Samaritan (Luke 10.30–37)

- the friend in need (Luke 11.5–13)

- the rich fool (Luke 12.15–21)

- the faithful and the evil servant stewards (Luke 12.35–48)

- counting the cost (Luke 14.25–33)

- the lost sheep (Luke 15.1–7)

- the lost coin (Luke 15.8–10)

- the lost son (Luke 15.11–32)

- the unjust steward (Luke 16.1–13)

- the rich man and Lazarus (Luke 16.19–31)

- the avenging of the oppressed widow (Luke 18.1–8)

- the ten slaves with ten coins (Luke 19.11–27)

In addition, one out of every seven passages from the Gospel of Luke is about money. But Luke is not just discussing money. He's helping God's people see how Kingdom economics are very different from the economics of the empire.

What I'm saying, and certainly what Luke is saying, is that caring for the poor is not some minor league truth to God. It's not a part of the "extras package" in the Christian life that you can decide to either take it or leave it. Luke is saying, "If you want to understand what Jesus stood for and why He came, it's found in his declaration of Jubilee."

Where Luke leaves off, the Book of Acts picks up. There's no question that those first century followers got the message. Not only did they get it, but they lived it.

In the Book of Acts, the early Church broke out of the prison of selfishness and truly began living with others' best interests at heart.

> *All the believers were one in heart and mind. No one claimed that any of their possessions was their own, but they shared everything they had. With great power the apostles continued to testify to the resurrection of the Lord Jesus. And God's grace was so powerfully at work in them all that there were no needy persons among them. For from time to time those who owned land or houses sold them, brought the money from the sales and put it at the apostles' feet, and it was distributed to anyone who had need.* (Acts 4.32–35)

Their actions were indicative of what the first century church practiced. It was God's economics, *distributing to any as they had need* (Acts 2.45; 4.35). The Church was being transformed. The greatest evidence of that transformation was the spirit of generosity that overtook the Church. People's hearts were being freed from the prison of selfishness. The Bible attributes this transformation to one thing; *God's grace was powerfully at work in them all* (Acts 4.33b).

Grace, and only grace, sets us free to love in this way. In our deepest poverty of spirit, God poured the wealth of heaven's treasure. He gave us Himself. He loved us in our brokenness, our messiness, and despair, and because we have experienced this transforming love, we discover new capacities to love others in the same way.

Apart from the grace of God, none of us can love in this way, and we are quite powerless to break free of the prison of self-focused living. Let's face it, practically everything in our world operates off of the principle of selfishness. It's humankind's default. So when God liberates the soul and frees us to move against our broken human nature, the world sits up and takes notice. Not only does it notice, but also, just like in the Book of Acts, the world wants what it sees.

God lavished grace on this community and broke their heart for the needy. This change was not forced on people, nor was it required of people. What people did, they did out of love. It's just what happens when people are gripped by Christ's love.

A little later, we're given a more intimate portrait of what Christ's expression of love looked like in the life of one individual.

> There was Joseph (the one the apostles nicknamed "Barnabas, the encourager." He was of the tribe of Levi, from the island of Cyprus). He was one of those who sold a field he owned and brought the money to the apostles for distribution to those in need. (Acts 4.36–37, Living Bible)

Barnabas was from Cyprus. Living in Cyprus, and being Jewish meant he had been living in exile from Palestine. The Palestinians called these exiled Jews Hellenists. Having lost their native Hebrew tongue, these Jews spoke only the Greek language. Barnabas was a Hellenist.

In those days, native Jews treated Hellenists more like Gentiles. They were considered less devout and often treated as second class. We see evidence of this mistreatment in the early Church when the Hellenistic widows were being neglected in the daily distribution of food while the Hebrew widows were not (Acts 6.1–4). It seems to be an obvious slight based on these cultural perceptions.

Barnabas may have faced similar treatment in his lifetime. It could be that he was looked down upon by his own people, but when the Palestinian Jews were in need, he sold his own property to provide for them. His hurts did not control him. Christ's love compelled him.

It's also worth noting that once he sells the property, he took the money and laid it all at the apostles' feet. His impulse was to give with no strings attached, allowing others the right to decide how best to use the money. His gift was not about control, ego, influence, or credit. It was just further evidence of a changed heart. It was a completely selfless act.

Of course, this amazing act of generosity is followed by an equally amazing act of selfishness. The story of Ananias and Sapphira is embarrassing. In light of everything that was happening, this story is the fly in the ointment. Their behaviors were totally out of sync with the work God was doing.

You see, God had been abundantly gracing His Church. People were spontaneously and generously sharing with one another. Jubilee was happening and happening out of love. God's vision was becoming a reality. His people were finally acting like His people, so much so that the Bible declares a startling fact - there were no needy people among them.

In a way, Ananias and Sapphira is a retelling of the Eden story. Like the Garden of Eden, the story involves a man and a woman, but this time the man is the first to sin and then followed by the woman. Their sin was the first sin recorded in the new Church, like Adam and Eve's sin was the first in paradise. In the same way, God had warned Adam and Eve, *When you eat from it you will certainly die* (Genesis 2.17), death also accompanied Ananias and Sapphira's sin of lying.

Ananias' name meant "Jehovah is gracious." Sapphira's name meant "beautiful." God had graced Ananias with a beautiful wife and material abundance, but in addition, the greatest grace of all was being loved by God and being included in the amazing community of the Church.

Although this couple had everything they could ever want, it was not enough. They wanted more. Maybe they wanted the attention Barnabas got for his gift. We don't know. From the outside, it appeared that they were following in Barnabas' steps, but unknown to most onlookers, they had secretly kept some of the proceeds from the sale of the property while claiming to give it all.

Their actions were really sad when you think how deceived they were. They had everything they needed but were convinced they needed more.

You and I are not all that different. We are graced by God, given what we need, but we convince ourselves (like Adam and Eve, like Ananias and Sapphira) that there's something else we have to have. Our selfishness is our undoing. Selfishness sabotages the work God is doing in community.

The lesson is that no environment on earth is so perfect, so graced by God that sin can't rear its ugly head. There is no gift that cannot be tainted by selfishness, and each of us can, of our own accord, willingly destroy paradise just to get what we want.

There was a similar story line repeated in Joshua 7.1–26. Remember when God's people entered Canaan, the Promised Land? This new land was so amazing that even today we still use the term "Canaan" synonymously with "Heaven."

Joshua's is another Eden story. The people of God are entering a new Eden called Canaan. God had given them His law and made clear His expectations. For forty years, He had taught them to depend on Him completely through the daily test of manna.

It was a new beginning, paradise regained, the culmination of their deliverance, and in this new paradise, there was just one major prohibition: All of Canaan belonged to them except for Jericho. The spoils of Jericho belonged to God. It was the first city they conquered, and as a result, it fell in the category of first fruit, and the first fruits always belong to God.

The problem was Achan. Achan committed the first recorded sin among God's people in Canaan. It was the sin of selfishness. He convinced himself that he has to have what he has been denied. He stole gold from Jericho and hid it in his tent. And just like Adam and Eve, just like Ananias and Sapphira, the day he sinned, he died.

There's a reason a version of this story is recorded at these three pivotal points of redemptive history. God is reminding us of the enemy that resides in the human heart. Its name is selfishness. Invariably, when selfishness wins, something always dies.

The common thread running through each of these stories is that selfishness invites the judgment of God. Selfishness is the very antithesis of what God is doing in the world. The work of God is manifested most powerfully in selfLESSness. Over and over in Scripture we see that the evidence of a changed heart is generosity; it's to have a heart like Barnabas, a heart that finds the need and fills it.

You see, it's not our big churches, our impressive weekend services, our sizeable budgets, or our superb communicators that best communicate what God is doing in the world. It really comes back to what Jesus said. He's watching for simpler expressions of the work of God than that. He's looking for a heart that shares a cup of cold water, clothing for the naked, bread for the hungry, and presence to the lonely. Jesus takes note of these simple acts of charity because His kids do these things when others won't.

Regardless of what you may think of Comedy Central's Stephen Colbert, few things register as deeply as his profound statement, "If this is going to be a Christian nation that doesn't help the poor, either we have to pretend that Jesus was just as selfish as we are, or we've got to acknowledge that he commanded us to love the poor and serve the needy without condition and then admit that we just don't want to do it." [6]

Chapter 9

BUT WE HAVE POOR PEOPLE RIGHT HERE!

ALTHOUGH YOU TAKE A VERY public stand acknowledging that you got it wrong, and even when you consistently lead in the new direction you are heading, there will always be those who don't get it. Call it "vision leak" or "erosion of purpose," but whatever term you use for it, know for a certainty that the vision and direction you stake out will need constant reinforcement.

At times, it will surprise you what objections are raised and who raises them. Because of these objections it is vitally important that you not only have clear direction from God, but also solid support from His Word for the things you are doing. Ever since my encounter with Oliver in the Soweto slum, God has been opening my eyes and illuminating my understanding to a treasure trove of wisdom in His Word surrounding mission to the poor.

Truthfully, a part of the reason I wrote this book is to help equip pastors with a compelling Biblical narrative that goes beyond a few "go-to" proof texts for mission. In fact, some of the stories you may already know have been misused and misappropriated for other purposes, but upon closer examination, they are really compelling missiological principles, much like the passage we'll be looking at in this chapter.

One objection that I have heard within my church (and others as well) is usually stated something like this, "We have poor people right here in America that we need to take care of first. Charity begins at home, you know."

Let's be honest, most people who make this claim are not genuinely concerned for the needs of the poor at home or abroad. More often than not, they are merely seeking a way to invalidate any charitable giving that extends beyond our borders, as if raising this objection excuses them from their obligation to address the needs of the poor anywhere.

X ❨When someone voices this objection to me, I say, "Great! Tell me about what you are doing to alleviate poverty in your own backyard."❩ Most often, the response you'll hear is deafening silence, or else a great deal of hemming and hawing as they reach back to some lame story about how one time they gave $20 to a homeless man.

I'm sorry, but I have no respect for those who try to excuse their apathy in this way. Those who are active and committed to combating poverty on the home front and abroad don't say such things. Besides, where in Scripture does it say that our national borders define the limits of our compassion? Where does the Bible say that addressing the needs of the Body of Christ ends with one's own neighborhood?

I'd be the first to admit that no one can say that they genuinely care about the poor while ignoring the poor right outside their own doorstep, but like I said, those raising this objection are usually doing little or nothing to help the poor anywhere.

Back in 1969, Francis Schaeffer wrote a book called *Death in the City*. In it, he invites the reader to imagine a world in which every child is born with a tape recorder around its neck. The device records only the moral judgments that people make in their lifetimes. For instance, every time this person says, "You were wrong in doing this, or you were wrong in doing that," the tape machine records that judgment and then switches off. Think for a moment about how often you yourself have made these judgments, probably literally thousands upon thousands of instances in your lifetime.

Then Schaeffer said to imagine that one day you die and stand before God, and God simply presses "play" and then listens patiently to this endless stream of judgments. Now imagine that the judgments you have made in this life become the standard by which you are judged in the next life. Imagine God saying to you, "If you knew it well enough to say it and apply it to others, I will now apply these same truths to you."

Schaeffer's explanation sounds eerily like Romans 2:1–3,

> Do you, my friend, pass judgment on others? You have no excuse at all, whoever you are. For when you judge others and then do the same things which they do, you condemn yourself. We know that God is right when He judges the people who do such things as these. But you, my friend, do these very things yourself for which you pass judgment on others! Do you think you will escape God's judgment? (Good News Bible)

When people object to helping the poor beyond their own backyards, what they're really doing is betraying the fact that they know the truth. They know they're supposed to be helping the poor, and because they know that truth well enough to pass judgment on others, God will rightly apply that same standard of truth to their life.

The next time you hear someone say, "We have poor people right here who need help," don't think of their statement as an indictment on those helping the poor overseas but as an indictment on the one who knows the truth well enough to apply it to others. In the end, God's question will be much like mine. "You were right. You knew you were supposed to be caring for the poor, so how did you care for them?"

I take no delight in relating this fact, and most certainly don't consider myself better than anybody else. I live with the knowledge that for many years I failed God miserably in this area. I relate these things because God said them, and the poor matter, regardless of where they live.

In addition, I don't do what I do, care like I care, or give like I give because I live in fear of judgment. Fear has nothing to do with what I do. I do what I do because God has set ablaze in my soul for the people of Africa and the poor in my community. Love compels me to care and give of my resources.

This is also a question we need to ask of the New Testament. Does God's Word say, "Charity begins at home?" or that we should be only caring only for those in our immediate context of relationships and those in nearest proximity?

To answer those questions, I'd like to highlight what has been called Paul's "obsession." Do you know what I'm referring to? This is something that Paul mentions in every one of his major letters to the Church. It's something that helped to unite the Gentile and Jewish Church, and it's the thing that led to his imprisonment, and ultimately to his martyrdom.

You might be tempted to say, "That's his preaching of the Gospel," but that's not it. The thing that's mentioned in every major letter, the thing that helped to unify the Church, and the thing that led to Paul's arrest and death was an offering. His "obsession" was an offering to support the poor saints in Jerusalem. The offering was no small matter to Paul. Not only does it occupy an important place in all of his major letters, but also Paul saw the offering as integral to the very mission of the Church.

Now, think about what Paul was doing. He was raising money in Gentile churches in foreign countries for poor people of another race in another part of the world.

I'd love to hear what Paul would say to someone who said, "Hey, Paul, charity begins at home. We have poor people right here we need to take care of first." Well, I don't have to wonder what Paul would say, because he answers this question explicitly in Scripture.

> Our desire is not that others might be relieved while you are hard pressed, but that there might be equality. At the present time your plenty will supply what they need, so that in turn their plenty will supply what you need. Then there will be equality, as it is written: "He who gathered much did not have too much, and he who gathered little did not have too little." (2 Corinthians 8.13–15)

What is Paul's point? The Body of Christ seeks equitable distribution of resources even across international borders. I love what Paul does to prove his point. He cites Scripture. That last quotation, *"He who gathered much did not have too much, and he who gathered little did not have too little,"* is from the Old Testament (Exodus 16.17–18).

It comes from the period of Israel's wilderness wanderings. It's talking about the time when God supplied His people with manna. As you may recall, every day the people had to gather the manna they needed for that day. Paul points out that the one *"who gathered much did not have too much."* You say, "Wait a minute. I didn't think you could over-gather the manna. I thought if you tried to hoard it, it would rot overnight." You're absolutely right. It was impossible to hoard manna. The only time it would not rot overnight was on the evening before the Sabbath. People could over-gather on Friday so as not to have to gather on the Sabbath day.

So what does Paul mean, those *"who gathered much did not have too much"*? What he's talking about is that because of physical aspects like age and ability, some were capable of gathering more than their fair share. Conversely, others, because of their age, ability, and health were not able to gather enough, but they didn't have *"too little."* It's obvious what Paul is saying: The reason everyone had enough is they shared.

Philip Hughes, in *The New International Commentary of the New Testament*, observed, "Some, such as those who were young and vigorous, gathered more than the prescribed omer; others, perhaps through age or infirmity, gathered less. But all that had been gathered was then put together and equitably measured out to each member." [1]

Be sure you get the main point: Able-bodied Israelites who were capable of gathering greater quantities of manna helped provide for the vulnerable ones who were not able to gather as much. In other words, if you were blessed with the capacity to over-gather, it was your responsibility to help those who could not do the same.

Also, remember, this sharing of manna happened in one place, at one time, among one people. But Paul now quotes this Old Testament Scripture as an example of what the Church is supposed to be doing in regards to this present crisis, but he doesn't apply it in one place among one people, like the mistaken notion of charity beginning at home. NO! Paul wrote this verse to say, "The Church that is comprised of Jew, Samaritan, and Gentile, and spread geographically from Palestine to Greece must do as they did."

Just like the over-gatherers in the wilderness, if a segment of the Body of Christ in this part of the world is blessed with the capacity to over-gather, it's for the sake of their brothers and sisters in other parts of the world who cannot do the same. The first-century Church put no national or geographical limits on charity. Borders, ethnicity, and locality do not define the Body of Christ, nor did they place limits on the extent of our compassion.

Consider this: If those *who gathered much did not have too much*, then there is such a thing as having "too much" in the economy of God. Where does God draw that line? I honestly don't know. But I do know this: To have much and not care about those who have gathered little is an indictment in itself. To be blessed with the capacity to over-gather and then give no thought to those who cannot breaks the heart of God.

You were blessed to be a blessing. You were given what you have in order to give out of what you have. To take the mentality "I got mine, now you have to get yours" is totally alien to the life we're called to live. Working hard to earn your money, being blessed by an unforeseen windfall, having good discernment, and making wise investments are all great things, but none of them excuse selfishness.

Listen again to Paul's teaching in light of all that…

> *Our desire is not that others might be relieved while you are hard pressed, but that there might be equality. At the present time your plenty will supply what they need, so that in turn their plenty will supply what you need. Then there will be equality, as it is written: "He who gathered much did not have too much, and he who gathered little did not have too little."* (2 Corinthians 8.13–15)

Paul is relating the way the Church is supposed to work. If the Church in one part of the world has a surplus, it's to help those in another part of the world who are struggling. Paul couldn't get any more explicit than that. The reason there is enough for everybody is because those who over-gather share with those who under-gather.

It reminds me of what Shane Claiborne said in his book *The Irresistible Revolution.* "God did not mess up and make too many people and not enough stuff. Poverty was not created by God but by you and me, because we have not learned to love our neighbors as ourselves." [2]

Abundance is supposed to be shared with those struggling in scarcity. It's a very powerful principle. The Body of Christ seeks equality. But there's more to this story.

God has many powerful lessons in the manna. His people had been delivered from years of generational poverty and oppression in Egypt. The people were, for the first time, facing life outside of that oppressive system that robbed them of their dignity and impoverished their lives and thinking. The Israelites had no idea what to expect, and there was deep fear in the unknown, so they complained.

Would that we had died at the Lord's hand in the land of Egypt, as we sat by our fleshpots and ate our fill of bread! (Exodus 16.3)

They wanted to go back to the way things were. They longed for Egypt. Life under Pharaoh was bad, but there were certain benefits to that system.

For His people to survive, God must teach them a new way of living and being in the world. He's going to teach them to live by His Kingdom priorities. And how would He do that? Primarily, God taught His people through the daily lesson of the manna. You see, manna was way more than just a feeding system. It was more than just a necessary food distribution apparatus. It was God's primary school. It's where God would teach the ABCs of His Kingdom's economics.

Manna was a teaching tool. It was a pattern to be emulated. It was the way God de-programmed His people from the ways of Egypt.

God gave His people some very specific instructions regarding the gathering of the manna (Exodus 16). These instructions went way beyond the simple process of gathering manna. He was schooling them in how to live according to His ways.

First, every family was instructed to gather just enough manna for its needs (Exodus 16.16-18).

Years of living in Egypt had scripted them in scarcity. They knew firsthand what it was like to never have enough. When you're used to never having enough, and suddenly there is more than enough, your greatest temptation is to hoard. Think about it. They had 400 years of reinforcement in this scarcity mentality. Their parents and their parents' parents, as far back as they could remember, had been totally dependent upon their masters to provide for their needs. The consistent themes after generations of slavery were lack, emptiness, and deprivation.

But in God's new economy, everyone would always have enough. Imagine how difficult it would be to break out of this scarcity mindset. When you are so used to not having enough, and suddenly there is abundance of bread, would you be tempted to over-gather? Do you think you might ever try to hoard some of the surplus? Might you ever worry that though the bread is there today, would it still be there tomorrow? How would your fears and your past and unpleasant experiences play with your mind and convince you that you needed more than God had provided?

Apply the first lesson of the manna to yourself. Do you ever think to yourself that there can be such a thing as having "too much"? When you are blessed with an overabundance, a bonus check, an inheritance, a raise, or a gift, does any portion of that blessing become a blessing for others? Or do you hoard it?

Have you ever had to go through an extended period of deprivation - a time of unemployment, medical bills that stacked up, or growing up in a family that struggled with addictions that nearly bankrupted the family financially? These things cause us to believe more in our personal fears than the promises of God. They tempt us to over-gather and worry about not having enough. We struggle with giving and caring for those with less because we never think we have enough.

(The second vital lesson contained in the manna was the prohibition concerning storing it up (Exodus 16.19–20).)

This principle alone is the very antithesis of Egypt's economic system. Do you remember how the Book of Exodus begins? It begins by telling us the reason the Israelites were being held as slaves…

So they put slave masters over them to oppress them with forced labor, and they built Pithom and Rameses as store cities for Pharaoh (Exodus 1.11).

Egypt, the super power, had conquered so many nations and had so plundered the wealth of these nations that they began to build mega U-Store-Its. Pithom and Ramases were store cities built to house the surplus goods pilfered from the wealth of alien nations.

God was schooling His people in behaviors opposite that of their captors. Egypt was all about accumulation. The Egyptians were the ultimate over-gatherers. Not only had Israel been subject to severe economic deprivation as they worked to build these store cities for Pharaoh, but they were also exposed to Egypt's ways. That approach to life looked far more attractive than theirs. It seemed far more secure and far happier with the endless accumulation of stuff.

Accumulation is a tempting thought and one that we easily succumb to. If I have become accustomed to not having enough, it is easy to fall into the trap of thinking that too much is better than not enough. But manna could not be stored. It rotted when placed in the U-Store-It.

The manna principle is what Jesus is referring to in the Sermon on the Mount when he says,

Do not store up for yourselves treasures on earth, where moths and vermin destroy, and where thieves break in and steal. But store up for yourselves treasures in heaven, where moths and vermin do not destroy, and where thieves do not break in and steal. (Matthew 6.19–20)

Endless accumulation will never lead to security. In God's Kingdom, the name of the game is SHARING, not ACCUMULATING. Ensuring that everyone in the community has enough is the path God blesses. Can't you see, based on the lessons in the manna, what is essential for life must be shared with everyone?

Our security is found in doing what God tells us to do. Our future does not rest in the ways of Egypt but in the ways of God. Are the ways of God anti-savings? No, absolutely not, but they are anti-hoarding, and it definitely flies in the face of the mentality that says, *Soul, you have many goods laid up for many years to come, take your ease, eat, drink and be merry* (Luke 12.19—New American Standard Bible). Real security is found in God and His ways.

3. [The <u>third</u> and final instruction God gave for His people concerning manna gathering was in regards to Sabbath rest (Exodus 16.22–30).]

On the seventh day, there was to be no gathering of manna. Here we find one of the most important principles for God's people to understand. God is the Provider. He is our Sustainer. God is Maker of the Manna, Author of Life, and Giver of Blessings.

The manna is God's manna, the fruit of His labor, and because it is God's fruit, it is our gift. The reason the people of God can rest from their endless striving, the reason they can set aside work and still know that their needs will be met, is ultimately they themselves do not secure their own blessings. God does.

X (We may work, but God gives the capacity to work. We may make great financial decisions, but God arranges the windfall.) Lest you forget, there are plenty of hard working, smart people in the world who don't have what you have. (You have what you have, and you are what you are because God made it so.)

The moment you forget God provides is the moment you forget the lesson of the manna. God's resources are not ours; they belong to God. As such, we can't hoard or monopolize any of them. Instead, I must learn to rest in the knowledge that I have a Provider in Heaven who knows what I need, knows what others need, and is providing abundantly for us all as long as we share.

There is always enough in the economy of God. With the world, X there is never enough. (Enough is a very important word to God.) It's a word that is virtually gone from our vocabulary and is even rarely heard in our theology.

Through the manna, God methodically taught His people His ways. His teaching stands in diametric opposition to practically every modern assumption we make about money and material security.

Today, if you use words "sharing" or "equality" in the context of money, as Paul did, there will be those who immediately try to pin a label on you. They will use words like "communist," "socialist," or "Marxist." What are those labels really about? Ignorance? Fear of God's truth? Or merely the reaction of a person whose true god is money? There's no getting around it; this truth is a full frontal assault to a belief system that elevates greed and selfishness.

Sadly, we are schooled in the ways of Egypt. Greed is the name of the game. Stockpiling and hoarding of resources is commonplace. Practically no one considers wealth a responsibility. We don't think like Jesus, who said, *"To whom much is given, of him shall much be required* (Luke 12.48).

Besides, what was going on in Corinth and throughout the New Testament was not communism, socialism, or Marxism. This teaching is not about the abolishment of private property. It's about recognizing God as the owner of all property. Paul did not force people to sell their possessions. What the Bible is describing is what happens voluntarily when people's hearts are gripped by the love of Christ. If you call their actions socialism, it's because you are ignorant of what socialism really is.

As a Christ follower, words like sharing and equality flow easily from our lips. If we believe in the truth and integrity of the Word of God, we must never shy away from the language it uses simply because ignorant people will try to shut you down. *"Let God be true and every man a liar"* (Romans 3.4).

This offering Paul collected in Gentile churches around the world for the poor in Jerusalem was very important to Paul. To show you just how important it was, let's look at what Paul had to say about it in Romans 15.

> *Thus I make it my ambition to proclaim the good news, not where Christ has already been named, so that I do not build on someone else's foundation, 21 but as it is written, "Those who have never been told of him shall see, and those who have never heard of him shall understand." This is the reason that I have so often been hindered from coming to you. But now, with no further place for me in these regions, I desire, as I have for many years, to come to you when I go to Spain. For I do hope to see you on my journey and to be sent on by you, once I have enjoyed your company for a little while. At present, however, I am going to Jerusalem in a ministry to the saints; for Macedonia and Achaia have been pleased to share their resources*

*with the poor among the saints at Jerusalem. They were pleased to
do this, and indeed they owe it to them; for if the Gentiles have come
to share in their spiritual blessings, they ought also to be of service to
them in material things. So, when I have completed this, and have
delivered to them what has been collected, I will set out by way of you
to Spain; ...* (Romans 15.20–28)

Paul's ambition was to preach the Gospel where it had never been named. That desire guided his life and fueled his passion, thus the reason when asked about Paul's obsession, you might be tempted to say, "Preaching the Gospel." The message conveys how Paul was wired-up, and it is unmistakable.

Furthermore, another reason why what he said here is so amazing and compelling, is Paul wrote this letter to the Romans from Corinth. If Paul wanted to go to Rome, if journey there fit with his holy ambition and God's purposes for Paul, why did he make a 1600-mile detour before heading on to Rome?

To go to Jerusalem is not just the opposite way; it's 800 miles in the opposite direction (round trip, 1600 miles). Rome is 600 miles the other direction, so he's actually closer to Rome than he is to Jerusalem. There has to be some compelling reason for this out-of-the-way, circuitous route. What is it that was right up there in importance with preaching the Gospel? Make no mistake about it. It was delivering this offering to the poor in Jerusalem.

Preaching the Gospel is of critical importance, and we all know that, but this journey to Jerusalem is a demonstration of the Gospel. It is the Gospel lived out. It is some of the most powerful evidence that there is that a people have been "gospel-ized." Without a doubt, when people move against stubborn selfishness, when hearts are freed to be generous, and when others matter just as much as self, then Jesus has come to take up residence in those hearts. The Gospel changes people. If there is no change, then we must quit calling it the Gospel.

What Paul's long, out-of-the-way journey underscores most is the ʔ (two sides of the Gospel: Preaching and demonstration. Preaching is of

vital importance, but so is demonstration. Proclamation without demonstration is only half a message.

For the integrity of the Gospel, Paul had to go to Jerusalem. In fact, I think the greatest mistake we make is in creating this dichotomy that somehow I can preach the Gospel without practicing it. Hand in hand, both halves represent the whole Gospel. Both are indispensible.

So when people say, "We have poor people right here," the answer is, "Yes, we do, and all over the world. Has your heart been broken for any of them? Has God freed your heart from the prison of selfishness and caused you to desire equality throughout the Body of Christ? Being blessed with a capacity to over-gather is a great privilege and respon- sibility. Who are the under-gatherers that God has called on you to bless? You believe the Gospel, but do you live it? Has your life truly been gospel-ized?"

Chapter 10

THE COMMANDMENT THAT EXPOSES THE HEART

J ESUS SPOKE TO THE ISSUE OF ECONOMICS MORE THAN ANY OTHER social issue. In fact, the Bible as a whole has a lot to say about money and the spiritual dangers associated with it, especially in the Gospel of Luke. Just peruse the parables in Luke: The two debtors, the rich fool, the tower builder, the unjust steward, the rich man and Lazarus, and the parable of the talents. Every one of these parables emphasizes a proper relationship with money.

Luke also explicitly records

(John the Baptist) *told them, "No more extortion—collect only what is required by law."* (Luke 3.13)

But woe to you who are rich, for you have already received your comfort. Woe to you who are well fed now, for you will go hungry. (Luke 6.24–25)

Watch out! Be on your guard against all kinds of greed; life does not consist in an abundance of possessions. (Luke 12.15)

The Pharisees really loved money. (Luke 16.14, Contemporary English Version)

There's no question, money is a powerful spiritual force. The New Testament even goes so far as to personify riches with the term ("Mammon," which means "that in which one trusts.") Anything in which we trust either is a god or becomes a god to us.

But Mammon is a different kind of god, and it's quite insidious. Its goal is to dominate your value system, your decision-making process, and your way of life without your personal awareness, so, typically, the person most under the influence of Mammon is least aware of it.

The influence of Mammon is the reason Jesus warns us about greed. It's not because it's worse than any other sin; it is more deceptive. The fact that this sin can capture our hearts and dominate our value systems without our awareness tells you just how deceptive it is, which is also why it is extremely rare, especially in church, to hear anyone confess that they struggle with greed.

Jesus once had an encounter that brings this truth home. He had a conversation with an affluent young man who asked him about eternal life. The key to understanding this story is a strategic omission on the part of Jesus. Read the story and see if you can spot what's missing.

> As Jesus started on his way, a man ran up to him and fell on his knees before him. "Good teacher," he asked, "what must I do to inherit eternal life?" "Why do you call me good?" Jesus answered. "No one is good—except God alone. You know the commandments: You shall not murder, you shall not commit adultery, you shall not steal, you shall not give false testimony, you shall not defraud, honor your father and mother." "Teacher," he declared, "all these I have kept since I was a boy." (Mark 10.17–20)

The guy asks Jesus, *What good thing must I do to get eternal life?* And Jesus says, *You know the commandments.* Then He lists them.

Jesus doesn't mention the first four commandments, but that's not the omission I'm talking about. The first four commandments address our relationship to God: No other gods before Him, no graven images, don't use His name in vain, and remember the Sabbath. Those are not mentioned in Jesus' list. Instead, Jesus emphasizes the last commandments that have to do with our relationship to our fellow man.

After Jesus enumerates those commandments, the young man answers confidently that he's met the requirements, so he says, "I've done them all. I've accomplished the list."

The one thing that very few commentators or preachers ever point out about this passage, but it is absolutely integral to understanding it, is (that of the six commandments that deal with our relationship to our fellow man, Jesus intentionally left out one.)

Now, when you find a list in the Bible and something is intentionally, purposefully left out, it should cause you to sit up and take notice. The one commandment Jesus left out was the very one that would most reveal this young man's heart. Jesus left out the tenth commandment, "Don't covet.")

What's peculiar about the commandments Jesus cites is that each manifests itself in a specific, external, observable behavior. If you murder, there is a body. If you lie, you've spoken something that others hear. If you commit adultery, you've committed a physical act. If you steal, you have in your possession something that belongs to another. Of course, we know that that is just a superficial reading of the law, and the law deals with intentions, not just actions.

But, if like this young man, you choose to read the law in a superficial way, you could interpret every command in such a way as to be outwardly compliant while remaining inwardly defiant; therefore, from an external point of view, (this guy thought he was being truthful. He had *"kept"* all of these laws from his youth.)

But what you can say about those commandments you cannot say about the tenth. Coveting is unique in that it addresses something unobservable. Coveting speaks exclusively to the heart. Having a lot of stuff doesn't necessarily mean you are guilty of the sin of coveting, and having virtually nothing doesn't render you guiltless either. In fact, you may be utterly poor, but coveting could have a vice grip on your heart. (Coveting is the one commandment that exclusively addresses the condition of our hearts.)

John Michael Talbot is the General Minister of the Hermitage, a community that belongs to a religious order called the Brothers and Sisters of Charity. Everyone in the group has relinquished all but the most necessary possessions. But Talbot once said something that I have found extremely revealing, "Taking a vow of poverty is not a cure for materialism.

Many people come to this community and go from being selfish with thousands of dollars to being selfish with a coffee mug." [2]

Talbot's statement reveals the problem with coveting. It's not about our stuff; it's about our attachment to the stuff. Our internal "wanter" is broken. It's that yearning to possess that lies at the heart of the problem. That's coveting.

Because coveting is unseen, it is easily denied; thus, the reason I said earlier that we rarely confess this sin. We're addicted to getting what we want, and just like an addict who denies the severity of his problem, we lie to ourselves about its control over our thoughts, spending, and peace of mind. We have difficulty admitting it to ourselves, to others, or even to God.

There is no question this young man who went to Jesus had a problem. His money, his stuff, mattered to him more than anything. No matter what he might try to tell himself, the truth was, money was his god. In light of the truth, he'd already broken the first commandment, to have no other gods but God. Martin Luther once said, "That to which your heart clings and entrusts itself is, I say, really your God." [3] This guy's god was his stuff.

What do you do when someone is living in denial about this fundamental reality? What if they want to know what is getting in the way of the life they were intended to live? Well, if you're Jesus, you give them what they're seeking.

> *Jesus looked at him and loved him. "One thing you lack," he said. "Go, sell everything you have and give to the poor, and you will have treasure in heaven. Then come, follow me." At this the man's face fell. He went away sad, because he had great wealth.* (Mark 10.21–22)

Nothing says more than this simple line, *"Jesus looked at him and loved him."*

Everything Jesus said to this young man was motivated by His deep love for him. Only someone who loves you incredibly will tell you when how you are living is standing in the way of what you most want in life.

(Only someone who loves you will dare break through your denial and ✗ help you clearly see the things that are holding you back) Jesus wants him to have God's best, so He gives him the truth in love.

There's a reason Jesus has focused on the commandments that relate to our fellow man. They are at the heart of this man's disobedience. Remember when Jesus summarized the teaching of the Old Testament law? He said the law was all about loving God and loving your neighbor. The truth is we can't honestly love our neighbor while simultaneously allowing greed to grow unchecked in our heart. Greed unchecked is what Jesus' challenge was all about, "Release the greed, give to those in need, follow me, and you will have the life you crave."

Jesus really loved him, as much as He loves you and me. Everything that stands in the way of freely and fully following Him has to go. Leave it behind. Give it up. Release it to others so that you can be untethered. When you come to Jesus asking what you need to do to have the life you truly crave, be ready for the answer He gives.

Most of us wouldn't ask of people what Jesus did, but that's because we don't love people the way Jesus does. We want people to think it's okay to be driven by the compulsive desire to possess, and we just add Jesus to that broken way of living. We do anything and everything we can to "take the edge off" this story so that people won't feel uncomfortable. For some reason, we think it's a bad thing for people to have to examine their own hearts or even ask themselves, "In what ways am I just like this young man?"

This story messes with us. It's unsettling. It makes us wonder, "Considering Jesus asked the young man once, might He ask it again? Might He ask it of me? Because that same brokenness exists in me. I know I have a broken wanter.

Instead of wrestling with an uncomfortable truth, I find myself searching for a reason to invalidate the story's application to my life. I scan the story for exceptions, exemptions, and exclusions for myself. This is that feeling of dissonance rearing its ugly head.

"Maybe Jesus is just exaggerating to make a point," I say to myself. (Sometimes even Bible scholars take this route. The term they use is

"Semitic hyperbole." They treat this exchange as an example of intentional exaggeration to make a point.

But that interpretation doesn't wash. Ask yourself, "Does anybody listening to this conversation think Jesus is just exaggerating? Does the young man hear hyperbole in the words of Jesus? Is the young man's reaction relief upon realizing that Jesus didn't mean to be taken literally?" Obviously, everyone in the story believes Jesus literally means what He says.

When I was a teenager, my preacher offered another alternative to this story. He said, "You don't really have to give everything up to follow Jesus; you just have to be willing to do that." And what he meant was, "You don't have to be willing, you just have to SAY that you're willing." I may have been young, but I was still smart enough to know that the guy in the parable didn't hear Jesus in that way. When he walked away, he left with the knowledge that he couldn't do what Jesus was asking. Therefore, the incident wasn't just about saying the right words or being willing to sell everything without actually being required to sell everything; the challenge was to do what Jesus asked.

Jesus did ask something audacious of this young man, and the young man couldn't do it. Does that mean He's asking the same of me? Of course He is. You can't serve God and Mammon. It's not possible. No other god can come before Him. If another god stands in the way, it's got to go. Why would anyone be exempt? None of the disciples were. All of them were asked to forsake all to follow Him.

The fact no one is exempted brings up an important point. What we seldom do when we read this story is stand in the rich young ruler's shoes. Instead, we turn this story into an either/or proposition. Either I am exactly like him (which very few people likely are), or I am nothing like him (which very few people likely are). Our intention is to invalidate the story's application to our lives.

I think, "If I can find an exception, such as I'm not rich or I'm not greedy, then this story doesn't apply to me." Even if your exceptions are true, you are not absolved of the need to wrestle with covetousness. Finding an exception doesn't let us off the hook for examining the degree to which these things are true of us. Even if we are not carbon copies of the rich young man, that doesn't automatically slide us into the category of those who have forsaken all to follow Him.

We need to be honest with ourselves. Here's what honesty compels me to do: Confess that I am more like the rich young man than I care to admit. Honesty forces me to say that I often find myself thinking how money would solve many of the problems I face. And it's money, having it or not having it, that makes far too many decisions in my life, instead of prayer and asking God what He wants. Coveting is something I find myself powerless to control. It rises unbidden in my heart. Whether it's a friend's new car, the next generation of technology, or a situation that seems far more desirable than my own, coveting is seldom far behind. I must come to terms with the reality that I have a broken wanter that I am quite powerless to control.

The rich young man is not the only guy in all the universe who ever struggled with this sin. He's not alone in getting caught up in materialism. He's not the lone individual who let his stuff get in the way of truly following Christ, and he is not the only one whom Jesus is ever going to ask to get rid of what holds him back.

Who is the rich young ruler? He's not a lying cheat. He's a sincere, moral man, the kind of guy you might hope to have as a business partner. He happens to be wealthy, and he's got a problem with coveting, but he is not Satan incarnate. Based on his own testimony, he's not the kind of guy who rips off his customers, cheats his employees, or doctors the books. He's a better man than many folks you will encounter in the business world.

Is this guy really that exceptional? No, he's not. His story is here for our benefit. It takes a ruthless honesty to see yourself in him and to see him in yourself. In fact, it is the only sure way to prevent this from happening to you. It is the sins we deny that yield the greatest power in our life. It is denial of this fundamental flaw that keeps it in the driver's seat.

The Bible tells us that the young man went away sad. Actually, that line is the only thing in this entire story that is hopeful. Yes, he walked away, but he walked away with clarity. He knew he had been shown a better way. He knew he'd been loved like no one had ever loved him before.

If you're going to walk away from truth and love, it's better that you walk away grieving about what you're leaving and knowing what you're walking away from. He knew what Jesus was offering was the better way; he just couldn't bring himself to sell all he had.

Coveting is a big deal in the Bible. It's the one sin that God uses most frequently to introduce us to ourselves. It's the original sin. In the garden, Adam and Eve didn't commit murder, lie, or steal. The sin they committed was coveting. They had everything they could ever want. Only one thing were they denied. What they were denied, they decided they simply had to have. That's the sin of coveting.

The Apostle Paul understood how God uniquely uses this sin to expose the human heart. He wrote in the Book of Romans,

X

Nevertheless, I would not have known what sin was had it not been for the law. For I would not have known what coveting really was if the law had not said, "You shall not covet." (Romans 7.7)

It's so easy to deny our depravity, especially when we define sin by its most egregious, outward expression, but when I see sin the way God sees sin, as something that begins in the heart, as something that has its origin in wanting what God has chosen not to give, my depravity becomes totally apparent. There is something undeniable about our broken wanter. I may hide it successfully from others, but its power and presence are obvious to me. It cries out for Christ's healing touch. It's the thing that causes me to live selfishly and disconnected from others in need.

Let's face it, none of us can be truly missional without facing the truth that in the same heart that bleeds for the poor and vulnerable, that there exists an enemy that excuses its own self-indulgence and convincingly says that nothing is more important than the self and its needs. It is extremely difficult to move others from a place of apathy to involvement if we ourselves are not intentionally examining our own hearts and yielding the brokenness we find to God.

Let me return to something I said earlier. We cannot honestly love our neighbor while simultaneously allowing greed to grow unchecked in our heart. Coveting is exaltation of self- need at the expense of God and community.

Ten is the number of completeness in the Bible. It's a number that suggests that nothing is lacking, that everything is in its proper order. Coveting as the tenth commandment suggests something more than merely the end of a complete list. There is something about the command that is unlike the others, that, in a sense, completes the others.

What did Jesus leave out of his list to the rich young man? He left out the tenth commandment. Jesus left out the one commandment that would most speak to this young man's shortcomings. Does not appear to make sense, does it? How could Jesus leave out coveting when it is the one commandment that would most reveal what this young man lacked? Well, maybe He didn't. Here are the commandments He did share.

- Honor your father and your mother.
- You shall not murder.
- You shall not commit adultery.
- You shall not steal.
- You shall not bear false witness.

Before we commit any of these sins, do we not first covet? My failure to honor my parents flows out of a desire to honor myself over either of them. When I murder, the value of your life is insignificant compared to my need for revenge or to get what I want. Adultery is the direct result of wanting a relationship that God has chosen not to give. Stealing so obviously has its taproot in coveting, and we lie to get what is not ours. All sin starts with wanting what I want more than I want anything else.

It is the most fundamental aspect of what it means to be a sinner. I covet. I want what I want. I want it more than I want what's best or right for you. I want what I want even when it isn't what God wants. In other words, I move against love for God and love for neighbor every time I covet.

What I'm saying is Jesus did confront this young man's deepest need. The young man just couldn't see how his coveting was getting in the way of loving his neighbor and God. He couldn't see how his love affair with riches was merely symptomatic of an orientation in his soul that was moving away from God and His desire for loving relationships.

Coveting moves in the opposite direction of love. We've talked about a lot of things in this book in regards to caring for the poor—the priority of caring for their needs, the expectation in the Church that those who can over-gather would do so for the sake of those who under-gather, that true religion provides for the widow and the orphan in their distress. However, the one thing that speaks convincingly to our spirit not to do those things is the internal, broken sin nature that wants what I want more than I want to help my fellow man.

You're not going to will that broken sin nature out of your life, and no list of rules will ever set you free. Trying hard not to be that way has an extremely limited shelf life. The only remedy for a broken wanter is love.

You see, there's a reason that Jesus, when asked about the greatest commandment, did not quote the Ten Commandments in their negative prohibitions. Instead, Jesus summarized all the Old Testament law in terms of God's positive righteous intentions: To love God supremely and love our neighbor as ourselves. To move in the direction of love is to move against our sin nature. We're to care for the poor and vulnerable among us because we love them, not because we've been commanded to or coerced into doing so.

Love will always do what a law never can. In this country, there are many laws that are intended to protect children in the home, laws that if violated can result in children being removed from the family and parents being prosecuted for their behavior. In all the years I have been a parent, I have never once been to the courthouse to read any of these laws, yet I am confident that I have kept every one of them. Do you know why? Because I love my kids, and because I love them, my actions toward them far exceed the letter of the law. I care for them as I care for myself, I love them like I love myself, and I willingly and happily sacrifice for them because they matter so much to me.

Imagine loving the poor, the vulnerable, and the marginalized like you love your own kids. Love for your children is the perfect definition of loving others the way we love ourselves. It shows us what that kind of loves looks like. It would mean going beyond what is required. Love like that would not just change a life, but ultimately it would transform the world. When love rules your life, your actions are guided by desire, not duty. "Ought to" motivation is replaced with "want to" motivation.

The law can be compared to the tiny circular mirror the dentist puts in your mouth when he's working. It helps him see cavities and the area where he is working, but he doesn't drill with the mirror, nor does he use it to pull teeth. It can show him the decay, it can show him what's wrong, but the mirror cannot provide the solution.

That's how the law works. It shows us what's wrong. It clearly exposes the problem and what is out of order in our life, but it is powerless to fix the problem. It's not the solution. The only solution is love.

Moving toward love is what sets me free from the vice grip of covetousness. Moving toward love enables me to think beyond my own individualistic needs and really to consider others' needs as important as my own.

The key to overcoming that selfish bent in the sinful nature is not trying harder to not be selfish, and you won't overcome it by constantly berating yourself that you should be more loving and less selfish. The key to overcoming selfishness is love. The reason we sacrifice and forgo personal needs for our spouse and children is love. Love has always been the key to overcoming selfishness.

In the light of sacrificial love, we have the key to an understanding that we can't love those we don't know. We don't fall in love with the nameless, faceless poor. To truly love someone, I must care enough to get to know them.

The first forays my church had in loving the poor came through the doorway of child sponsorship. It was vitally important to teach the church that for sponsorship to be transformative, it had to be more than a transaction. If all one did was sign up for an automatic debit or credit card charge without making any attempt to know the child, then the amazing side of child sponsorship would remain unrealized. Of course, the work in the community would be funded, and I'm not trying to minimize the importance of funding, but what our people needed most was a relationship with people in poverty.

In presenting child sponsorship as an opportunity to move out of our comfort zones and get to know and love a child in need, an unintended consequence occurred. Truly, something I didn't anticipate happened. Loving vulnerable children opened the heart of the church to loving all people everywhere. The ethnic diversity of our church began to grow exponentially. People from all walks of life, from every social group, and from diverse sides of the political spectrum, even the homeless, were finding a home and a family among us. Today, when outsiders remark how diverse Springcreek is, it warms my heart to say, "It looks like the family of God."

It's unmistakable in Scripture that God has a huge heart for vulnerable ones. His love for them is real, His prioritizing of them not debatable, and His desire that we do the same is unmistakable. If we are having trouble loving the poor as God does, it's largely because we don't see them as He sees them. Pray to be given His eyes that see beyond rough exteriors. Pray to have His heart that refuses a narrative that demonizes the poor. Pray for the willingness Christ had to enter into poverty in order to transform it, and pray for His love that will stop at nothing to make sure that every soul knows they matter to Him.

Chapter 11

A VISION FOR LITTLE BARNS

THERE'S A TEACHING IN LUKE'S Gospel that gets to the heart of this disconnect we have between our blessings and our responsibilities. Jesus was teaching, a crowd had gathered, and someone abruptly interrupted Him mid-teaching.

> *Someone in the crowd said to him, "Teacher, tell my brother to divide the inheritance with me." Jesus replied, "Man, who appointed me a judge or an arbiter between you?" Then he said to them, "Watch out! Be on your guard against all kinds of greed; life does not consist in an abundance of possessions."* (Luke 12.13–15)

It was an odd request. It was obvious that this man is not really seeking advice and really doesn't have a question for Jesus. He was embroiled in a dispute with his brother, and he wanted Jesus to take his side. He was not seeking reconciliation with his brother; he was not asking, "What's the right thing to do?" In his mind, he'd already got that figured out. He just wanted Jesus to rubber stamp his idea of justice.

But Jesus refused to be drawn into this mess. Instead, he said, *"Man, who appointed me a judge or an arbiter between you?"*

You say, "I thought matters of justice were a big deal to Jesus. Why does He seem so unconcerned about this man's cry for justice?" Jesus was not unconcerned. It was just that there was a bigger issue at stake. The man didn't need Jesus to take his side. Trying to hammer his brother into submission by saying, "The Rabbi Jesus told me to tell you to divide the inheritance," was not going to get to the heart of the matter.

What this man desperately needed was someone to know him so well and love him so deeply that they would speak to the real need behind the request. Jesus is that person Who knows and loves us like that.

Jesus could see the greed behind the request, and it was greed that lay at the heart of this feud. Greed was driving the brothers apart and fueling their dysfunctional patterns of relating.

Jesus gave the man truth in love. But first, He turned to the crowd and issued a warning. Let everyone who had heard this request beware, for the same thing can happen to any of them. Jesus told them, *"Watch out! Be on your guard against all kinds of greed. A man's life does not consist in the abundance of his possessions"* (Luke12.15).

This is Jesus' line in the sand. Greed is a craving, a longing, for what God has chosen not to give. It's the age-old sin of covetousness. It's the original sin. Solomon saw it as the line of demarcation between the righteous and the unrighteous. *"All day long he craves for more, but the righteous give without sparing"* (Proverbs 21.26). In Solomon's view, you are either a hoarder or a giver; you are either unrighteous or righteous. It's your attitude toward accumulating or sharing that determines your righteous standing with God.

But to Jesus' larger point, even if you could amass an abundance of possessions, it's still not going to result in the life you really want. You and I were made to crave for the life God gives, the life that satisfies. That's what the Greek word for life (zoe) in this verse actually means, "life that satisfies." That kind of life doesn't come from your inanimate stuff. It comes from God.

Our stuff will not bring us the life we crave, because there is no life in stuff. By the way, this is the reason the Church must rethink its missiological approach. In America, we think the poor are poor because they lack stuff, so we decide the best way to help the poor is to give them stuff, a kind of "salvation by stuff." But stuff has not produced life in us any more than it will produce life in them. Materialism is an attempt to find our life and happiness in material goods. It is an utterly futile way to live. When we turn missions into adventures in giving away stuff, what we're really doing is giving away our misery and nothing more.

Vicki Baird, Director of MercyWorks with the Vineyard Church, says, "The poor need relationships more than they need money. In the inner city, there's a lot of free stuff to be had. What the poor need are people who care." [1]

Now Jesus was going to get to the heart of the brokenness in the young man who had come demanding that his brother divide the inheritance with him. Following the initial warning in Luke 12.15, he tells another story about a man who is blessed with abundant stuff (in this case, a bumper crop).

> And he told them this parable: The ground of a certain rich man yielded an abundant harvest. He thought to himself, "What shall I do? I have no place to store my crops." Then he said, "This is what I'll do. I will tear down my barns and build bigger ones, and there I will store my surplus grain. And I'll say to myself, 'You have plenty of grain laid up for many years. Take life easy; eat, drink, and be merry.'" (Luke 12.16–19)

His warning was about how abundant stuff will never produce life.

Now, I'm sure the farmer Jesus described was a hard worker. Like every farmer, he planted, he weeded, and he harvested. Given the fact that he was already rich, even before this bumper crop, we might even surmise that he's a savvy businessman and had handled his investments well.

Even though the man appeared to be blessed, Scripture is clear—no one succeeds on his or her own. In Matthew 5.45b we learn, *He (God) causes his sun to rise on the evil and the good, and sends rain on the righteous and the unrighteous.* It is God's blessing of sunshine and rain that makes the crops grow. God causes seeds to germinate and allows them to multiply. No one can ever say that what they have is solely the result of their own effort. Hard work alone is never the full explanation for anyone's success, because even the very abilities we have are a gift from God.

> You may say to yourself, "My power and the strength of my hands have produced this wealth for me." But remember the Lord your God, for it is he who gives you the ability to produce wealth... (Deuteronomy 8.17–18a)

No human being can claim credit for all the good things that happen in their life apart from insulting their Maker.

What's true of the rich man in Jesus' story is also true of us. Much of what we have and what we are was given to us. There were certain gifts that came with birth.

Where you were born and whom you were born to are things absolutely beyond your control but have significantly shaped the trajectory of your life.

Imagine if you'd been born in western Kenya and there were schools that you could attend for free, but the school required a uniform, and your parents were too poor to purchase one. Or what if you had lost both of your parents to disease, and you became your sibling's sole provider at the age of nine? Even doing your best with marginal reading and math skills, what would you hope to accomplish, given your limitations? What if you lived in a place where only a fraction of the kids actually completed high school? What if you had a nearly zero chance of ever going to college? If you were born into one of these situations instead of the place where you were born, where would you be today?

Regardless of where we live, God has provided for us all. He has given us the ability to do whatever we're doing. Just like the farmer in the parable, there are many things we've been given that led to our success.

Our Christian worldview informs our understanding of this story. The farmer's success was not completely his own doing, but evidently he must have believed that it was, because he makes no acknowledgement to God and gave absolutely no thought for other people. His worldview is entirely egocentric. He spoke and acted as one who sincerely believed that "he himself" was the source of this amazing abundance.

This blessing was so large that he could then think of retiring with ease and living off his savings for the rest of his life, but he never said a word about how he could help those less fortunate. Evidently, that never entered his mind. Instead, all he thought about was how to capture and hold onto this mega blessing all for himself.

Wealth is a blessing, it truly is, but nowhere in God's Word are God's blessings seen as something we hoard or keep for ourselves. We're blessed to be a blessing. To whom much is given, much will be required. In the Bible, wealth is not coupled with PRIVILEGE; it's coupled with RESPONSIBILITY.

There's one line in Jesus' story that speaks volumes, *"He thought to himself..."*

No doubt that one line would have perked the ears of Jesus' listeners. This guy was alone, disconnected. He was not in community. Instantly, what comes to mind is the man the prophet Isaiah spoke of, *"Woe to you who add house to house and join field to field till no space is left and you live alone in the land."* (Isaiah 5.8) Isaiah is warning the rich who add blessing to blessing, increase their land and their holdings to the point that they are left alone in the midst of their wealth. You can build your little empire and increase your living space so much that you find yourself alone in the "Kingdom of Me."

(In other words, selfishness breeds isolation.) That's what Isaiah is saying. Smaller spaces are shared spaces, but the more we increase our square footage, the more isolated we become. That's where this rich man is. He's alone with no one to talk to but himself.

Dr. Kenneth Bailey has written an excellent book called *Jesus Through Middle Eastern Eyes.* Bailey is excellent in describing cultural nuances of Biblical stories that the untrained would miss. For this story, Bailey writes, "This is a very sad scene. In the Middle East, village people make decisions about important topics after long discussions with their friends. Families, communities, and villages are tightly knit together. Everybody's business is everybody else's business. Even trivial decisions are made after hours of discussion with family and friends. But this man appears to have no friends. He lives in isolation from the human family around him, and with an important decision to make the only person with whom he can have a dialog is himself" (p.303) [2]

There was no one in his life who knew him so well and loved him so much to tell him the truth. There was no one close and connected, no one who was such a good friend that they would help him see how incredibly selfish he was being.

χ (If you live your life disconnected from a world of need, it's easy to be _selfish._)In fact, it's your default. If you are isolated and insulated from people who are hurting and hungry, their needs will never be a factor in any of your decisions. If you have not intentionally placed yourself in community with those less fortunate, then all that will ever matter to you is how to maximize life's blessings for yourself.

In today's society, we don't think of similar wealthy people as being wicked or evil or uncaring. We say, "They're successful, their ship came in, or they've arrived." We think if someone has been rewarded with superabundance, then that's their ticket to Easy Street. We envy them, but we don't think of them as evil people. In that way, we are just like the Rich Fool.

God doesn't bless us just so we can get and keep more stuff. Material blessing is for you and your community. Just like we learned with the lesson of the manna, those blessed with the capacity to over-gather have been given that privilege for the sake of those who under-gather. The sick, the elderly, the disabled, and those suffering under oppression need us. They need the people of God to factor them into their financial decisions. God's people, by virtue of the fact that they are God's people, think differently.

Dr. Klyne Snodgrass, professor of New Testament Studies at the North Park Theological Seminary, said, "Foolishness consists in thinking that responsibilities ends with securing one's own economic future." [3]

Now you're beginning to see the parallels between the rich man and the young man who came to Jesus demanding our Lord take his side in this inheritance dispute. That man's underlying problem was greed. He was every bit as greedy as the rich farmer in Jesus' story, which is why Jesus told him the story.

X (*But God said to him, "You fool! This very night your life will be demanded from you. Then who will get what you have prepared for yourself?" This is how it will be with whoever stores up things for themselves but is not rich toward God. (Luke 12.20–21)*)

Jesus couldn't be any more explicit than He is in this verse. Storing up riches for yourself is the very antithesis of what it means to be rich toward God. Those who hoard blessings are not rich toward God. Those who have been blessed and then use those blessings in selfish ways are not rich toward God. Those principles are what the story illustrates, and that's Jesus' conclusion; therefore, the converse must also be true, that being rich toward God is all about turning wealth and material blessing into an avenue of blessing for others.

Eugene Peterson said, "Building a barn is normal work for a farmer. No one would ever think of it as a moral failure. No farmer ever got in trouble by his pastor or put in jail because he builds a barn. The story of the barn builder doesn't condemn. It just sits there in our imaginations. So it makes us wonder. Did the brother who asked the original question wait around in the crowd long enough to get it? Or because it had never occurred to him to ever build a barn, did he impatiently walk away and continue to shop around the neighborhood for another rabbi who would take up his cause?" [4]

Building bigger barns really seems like such a benign thing to do. In fact, I would imagine that all of us can think of a time when we have done something similar. Some huge blessing came our way, and we made sure that we maximized the benefit for ourselves. It's easy to do. It's easy to come up with convincing rationale for bigger barns. In a world where bigger is always better, many of us don't pause long enough to think about the cost. Yes, we can have bigger barns, but at what cost? Not just personal cost in terms of time, energy, money, or stress, but does our bigger barn come at another's expense?

Some years back, we experienced a real buyer's housing market in Texas. You could get into a really nice home for a fraction of its actual value. My wife and I were living in a smaller-than-average home at the time, and the thought of upgrading our home, having more space, and being in a community where home values were very stable was extremely appealing to us.

So I bought a house that was nearly twice the size of our present home. It was the corner lot. It was gorgeous. It was listed below market value.

In addition, this house was held by a corporation. The corporation had bought the house from one of its employees so they could relocate him to another part of the country. At the time we were looking at the house, they were very motivated to unload the property.

I told myself, "This house will enhance my ability to do ministry. I can have more people over. I'll be a better steward because the value of this property is so much more stable than my old neighborhood."

There was a measure of truth to all of that, but even at a bargain, my mortgage payment nearly doubled. The heating, cooling, maintenance, and taxes were also considerably more than they had been with my prior house. In all, this amazing deal added a great deal of stress to my life and worry over the additional expenses. What I learned in my "bigger barn" was that wanting more and getting more did not produce more life.

I thought I would be so happy when I first bought my great big house on the corner lot in the golf community; in truth, I was much happier three years later when I sold it and purchased another house, smaller than my original home and at half the price of the big house.

It cost me a great deal personally, but all those extra dollars poured into mortgage, taxes, and utilities are all gone now. It was money I wasted and can never get back. I wish I could say I learned my lesson so well that I never made that mistake again. The truth is I continue to learn the lesson in big ways and small that my personal quest for "bigger barns" is the one way I most frequently rob from the Kingdom of God.

This man who went to Jesus insisting that He take his side in the inheritance dispute could not see how greed was destroying his relationship with his brother, any more than the Rich Fool could see how building bigger barns was moving in the opposite direction of loving his community. Although it took some time, I eventually realized that my bigger barn was hurting me and everyone I loved.

One of the things that makes this parable unique among all the parables Jesus ever told is that this is the only one in which God becomes an actor in the story. God actually interrupts the man's self dialog and speaks the verdict on the man's life. *This very night your life will be demanded from you* (Luke 12.20a). It's also the only parable where a life was demanded back. The verdict is serious stuff to God. To be blessed and act in selfish ways in regards to that blessing leads to the ultimate product recall. God says, "This is not what life is about. This is not why I made you. This runs counter to the original manufacturer's specifications. This product, your life, is defective and must be recalled."

(The Greek word for "demand" is the word *apaiteo*, which literally means to recall or demand something back. The point is our lives are on loan. God lent you your life, and because He lent it to you, it's His legal right, at any time and for any reason, to demand it be returned to Him. Nothing belongs to you. Everything you have and everything you are is borrowed.)

The fool did not understand the concept of borrowed possessions. He lived his life in fundamental denial of this reality. His surplus was not really his to do with as he wished. It was God's surplus and must be distributed according to His kingdom priorities. His life was not really his to do with as he pleased. It, too, was on loan to him from God to be invested in God's purposes.

I think this is why Eugene Peterson translated the last verse in the parable like this:

> *That's what happens when you fill your barn with Self and not with God.* (Luke 12.21)

These are unsettling truths, aren't they? It's obvious that the lesson was a big deal to Jesus, the cost being a man's life. When do you cross the line? How do you know if your barn is too big? How much can I keep for myself? And how much am I required to give away? We want specifics. We want to be told, "Here's the rule, and as long as you give 'X' amount or 'Y' percentage, everything is cool with God."

But the story doesn't give us any details like that, does it? It makes clear that you can't keep it all, but it says nothing about how much you are to give away. Like Eugene Peterson says, "It just sits there." And because it sits there, we engage in the game of exceptions and exemptions.

We tell ourselves, ("But I have to take care of myself first.) If I don't do that, I won't have anything to give./ Can't you see how that line of

(what my dad said to me — you have to take care of yourself nobody else will) reasoning completely misses the point? Jesus didn't tell us this story to prioritize taking care of ourselves. He related the story to free us from the prison of constantly prioritizing ourselves. Our default is always to prioritize ourselves, but God wants to teach us to love.

This story is the antithesis of self-absorption. If we are to live out the Gospel, then we must cease with the self-justification. If you know that selfishness is an area where you struggle, it is far better just to admit that it's a part of your life that stands in need of redemption. Admit that it's a part of your life where you struggle to find God as your source of security instead of stuff, because in that admission, you set in motion a process that culminates in the healing touch of God. Your admission of need doesn't repel God; it melts Him. He has a special place in His heart for desperate people. Own your struggle, but don't excuse your struggle. Confess your struggle, but don't justify your struggle.

I think this story Jesus tells lacks specifics for a reason. Love doesn't follow rules; it follows God. God wants us to live our lives loving Him with all our heart, soul, mind, and strength, and He wants us to love our neighbors as ourselves. The Kingdom of God turns on the axis of love. That understanding changes the question altogether.

The question is not "How little can I do and still be okay?" And the question is not "What do I have to do?" What God wants to do is set us free to ask, ("What would love have me do?")

The answer to that question is as different as the myriad of need we will encounter in life. Sometimes, because of love, we will give it all (like the little boy who surrendered his sack lunch to Jesus in John 6). And sometimes, because of love, we will allow the other to choose what they want (like Abraham offering Lot the choice of land in Genesis 13). There might even be times where in love I don't have anything to give, but I give something better (like Peter with the beggar in Acts 3). There's no rule that covers all those situations, only love.

(You see, love listens and love learns. Love never takes a cookie-cutter approach to people or situations.) There is no one-answer-fits-all as it relates to people, for every situation is unique. Each one requires an investment of love that will lean into the situation to listen and learn. What God would have us do is partner with Him in loving the world as He does.

What would it be like for God's Church to catch a vision of "little barns," instead of thinking "more for me" or "how big can I build my empire?" What if we asked, "How can we multiply barns so that everyone has one?"

There's a guy in my church named Mike Bencheck. He is a great guy and a successful businessman. As a manager with a high-tech company, he can afford to live a better life than the average person, but God gave Mike a vision for "little barns."

Suburban America is seeing a huge uptick in the homeless ranks in their communities. With the availability of mass transit, many of the homeless find that the suburbs are a safer alternative to the inner city.

A few years ago, about the time our church started down this path of transformation, God gripped Mike's heart for the homeless, so instead of building a bigger and better lifestyle for himself, Mike intentionally downsized his life. He did it because it freed him financially to buy small starter homes, houses that could easily serve as transitional living spaces for the homeless. Mike is not into building bigger barns; he's into making sure everyone has a barn of his own. That's Kingdom living!

Over 1,700 years ago, St. Augustine of North Africa said about the Rich Young Man, "He (the rich fool) did not realize that the bellies of the poor were much safer storerooms than his barns." [5] That's a vision for little barns. If you want a good place to store your excess, it's in the bellies of those who are empty. If you have more than you need, how about blessing those who need more than they have?

I believe the Church needs to recapture a vision for little barns. Bigger is not better. For the Church to fall into the trap of "more" (just like our culture) is not a good thing. Many of our churches already have more than what they need. If the Church is constantly building "bigger barns," have we not become rich fools?

To take Jesus literally in all that He says about the rich farmer is extremely painful. To take Him seriously is how He appraises a life and causes us to question everything about our lives and choices.

What would happen if the Church in America quit building bigger barns? What if we quit the whole business of empire building, with franchises of our unique "brand" of church in every neighborhood, and instead started empowering and resourcing the Church that exists in struggling communities?

What if we believed that God had blessed our churches to over-gather for the sake of those churches that under-gather? What if the blessings that came our way as spiritual communities were seen as ways to bless other churches? I'm talking about a true Kingdom perspective that sees beyond yours, mine, and ours.

What if, instead of building ever-increasing church campuses (read "bigger barns"), we began making investments in the church that exists in underserved, under-resourced areas of our city? What if we helped them, came alongside them, and built their capacity, so they were given what they need to be change agents in their neighborhood?

X (What if we did all these things without taking over? What if we did it out of love?)

What if we believed that those who already have a primary stake in their community were more effective agents of change than outsiders coming in? What if we believed that God was not calling us to do easy things, but difficult things, impossible things that required His help? X What if we quit empire building and started Kingdom building? What if we got a vision of little barns?)

Chapter 12

A YARD FROM THE GATE OF HELL

CHARLES STUDD, WHO SERVED FOR years with the China Inland Mission, once said, "Some want to live within the sound of church or chapel bell; I want to run a rescue shop within a yard of hell." [1]

That statement has always stuck with me. There has always been a part of me that hungered, like Charles Studd, for service on the frontlines. I wanted to be on duty at the last point of hope. When I imagined where that would be, I usually thought some urban jungle, or else a quite literal jungle on the backside of nowhere. To me, a yard from the gate of hell meant something totally foreign to the life I had always known. In my mind, it was the shadiest, darkest place I could imagine far away from my sheltered suburban existence.

But I was wrong about what that place would look like and wrong about where that place would be. When you look at Christ's teaching about hell, it's not the sinners, tax collectors, prostitutes and other notorious bad guys that Jesus regularly warns of the dangers of hell fire. It's the religiously comfortable and the judgmental. These people are far closer to hell's gates than others.

I've come to understand what Jesus knew: The truly broken of this world are often the most receptive to the Gospel. It's only the broken who are in touch with their desperate needs, it's only the sick who know they need a doctor, and it's only in acknowledging that we are sinners that we cry out for a Savior.

The self-sufficient (the competent and complacent), however, are not in touch with that same neediness. They think they're just fine the way they are. It is this group who stands precipitously near the brink of hell.

Truly, a yard from the gate of hell is better represented by the edge of my manicured lawn in suburbia than the curb of the Union Gospel Mission downtown.

If you take Jesus seriously about what endangers the human soul, there's no other conclusion that can be reached. We are most likely to forget about God when we're full of ourselves. It's not the guy who knows he's a sinner that is in the greatest danger. It's the guy who looks at the sinner and says, "Thank God, I'm nothing like him!" According to Jesus, it's the self-righteous man who walked away from God's house un-justified (Luke 18).

But there is hope. There is hope even in communities that have lost touch with their own spiritual reality. We can see this hope in the New Testament in a community called Laodicea.

Laodicea is the last church in the seven that Jesus wrote to in the Revelation. It's the last church, and it's the worst church. It was a wealthy community, a town filled with large entertainment complexes, theaters, a huge stadium, lavish public baths, and fabulous shopping centers. There were even a lot of large, beautiful homes, the ruins of which are still vis-ible today. Really, for all intents and purposes, it is the one community in Revelation most like modern-day suburbia.

Laodicea had a problem. Jesus tells us plainly in Revelation 3…

You say, "I am rich; I have acquired wealth and do not need a thing." But you do not realize that you are wretched, pitiful, poor, blind and naked. (Revelation 3.17)

The saddest thing about Laodicea is not the fact that they were "*wretched and miserable and poor and blind and naked.*" It's the fact that they didn't realize they were in such sad shape. They thought they were rich, yet they were wretchedly poor. They thought they were healthy when they were really sick. They were a spiritual mess and ignorant.

To make matters worse, they went further and claimed, "We don't need a thing." They underestimated their brokenness while inflating their own sense of goodness.

It's sad that those first to criticize, first to get up on their moral high horse, are usually the ones most disconnected from their own moral failures.

It's hypocrisy, but the hypocrites are unaware of it because they are disconnected from their own wretchedness, poverty, and blindness. They don't believe they share the deficiencies of others. They are above those deficiencies, seemingly in need of nothing and no one.

Jesus digs further into the sin of the affluent church,

I know your deeds, that you are neither cold nor hot. I wish you were either one or the other! So, because you are lukewarm—neither hot nor cold—I am about to spit you out of my mouth. (Revelation 3.15–16)

It's peculiar that Jesus wished they be either cold or hot. I totally understand His desire for them to be hot. Who wouldn't rather deal with those who are "on fire" for God? However, why would Jesus prefer coldness to lukewarmness?

To be cold, in our minds, makes a person unreachable, but there is actually no one harder to reach than the lukewarm. It's far easier to win a whore, a hardened criminal, or a stone-cold atheist than the lukewarm. It's far easier to reach the outcast, the prostitute, and the wretched than to reach a Pharisee.

Jesus said, "I would rather have you cold than lukewarm. I'd rather you be a sinner who knows he's wretched and broken than a sinner who thinks he's okay. I'd rather you be a broken man, eyes cast to the ground, beating on your chest saying, 'God, be merciful to me, a sinner' than a Pharisee who prays, 'God, I thank You that I'm not like other men.'" When God gets a taste of our lukewarmness, it's so distasteful that it makes Him sick.

When you are lukewarm, God is more like an obligation, another item on your checklist than the Center around which your whole live revolves. When you're lukewarm, you ask, "What do I have to do?" versus "What would love have me do?" We give God the bare minimum, just enough to placate our conscience, but not enough to make a difference. In the words of Brennan Manning, the author of the Ragamuffin Gospel, the lukewarm get "...just close enough to God to warm themselves with His love but not close enough to be consumed by it."

Things were bad in the Laodicean church, but not beyond repair. And God won't give up without a fight. After speaking the truth to His church, in hopes that they would see it and own it, He turned with tenderness toward them.

> I counsel you to buy from me gold refined in the fire, so you can become rich; and white clothes to wear, so you can cover your shameful nakedness; and salve to put on your eyes, so you can see. Those whom I love I rebuke and discipline. So be earnest and repent. Here I am! I stand at the door and knock. If anyone hears my voice and opens the door, I will come in and eat with that person, and they with me. (Revelation 3.18–20)

Here Jesus refers to His Church as *"those whom I love."* God speaks only the hard truth about our condition to wake us up and bring us back. When God rebukes us, it should really make us feel loved. If He didn't care, He would just walk away, but even in all our half-hearted, lukewarm condition, Jesus never gives up on His love for His Church.

Jesus invites us back to fellowship with Him. There are no demands here, just a request, "Will you let me back into the center of all things where I belong?" He will never burst through the door. He waits to be invited. Or in the words of A.W. Tozer, "Complacency is a deadly foe of all spiritual growth. Acute desire must be present or there will be no manifestation of Christ to His people. He waits to be wanted." [2]

In Laodicea and in churches like it that lose touch with their personal and spiritual brokenness, Christ found Himself locked out. He wanted desperately to be invited back in. Do we even know that He's been shut out?

The suburban lifestyle can be hazardous to our followership. It is far more likely to breed lukewarm commitment than passionate discipleship. Whether intentionally or not, we often communicate the message that we can simply "add" Jesus to our already messed up value system and then return to business as usual.

X (As a result, we are most likely to "spiritualize" verses we should be "actualizing.")We are most likely to say, "Not everyone is called to this," then use that as a carte blanche excuse to never even consider the claims of the Gospel on our personal lifestyle. We give ourselves an out, a rationalized, believable argument that justifies our over-accumulation at the expense of others.

Yes, Africa was a wrench in the works for me. The day I met Oliver in the Soweto slum was the beginning of a revolution in my life. It is far from over. In loving the poor, God has slowly but systematically and un-relentingly stripped the blinders from my eyes. The implications for my suburban existence are staggering. Even as I write these words, there is this acute awareness in me that this revolution is far from over. There are many difficult questions that I still cannot answer. There are implications I haven't even begun to ponder. There are ways this affects the way I lead, forcing me to look within and ask, "How true is any of this about my own life today?"

The one thing I do know is that I cannot get ahead of God. His word to me is always the same, "Just match my pace." I want to stay in lock step with the Spirit of God, and I want to go willingly wherever He tells me to go. He gives me truth as I can handle it. He gives me truth as I accept it and abide by it.

It's tempting at this point in the book to offer you some kind of for-mula, some recipe for the transformation of your church, but I can't do that, nor will I do that. Followers don't need formulas.

It's important that you spend time on your knees and enter into a process of discernment with your leaders about where God is taking you. Then take that first step, whatever it happens to be. Once you've taken that step, you'll be in a better position to receive more guidance, for that's the way God always guides, incrementally, by showing us the next right step.

Honestly, I think we get so caught up in thinking that we want to be a part of the next "BIG" thing God is doing that we forget God's prefer-ence for little things, small voices, and the most inauspicious of circum-stances. When I look back over the last six years, every major thrust for-ward and every revelation of profound truth has come through simple circumstances and ordinary people.

For me, this journey constantly reaffirms the wisdom of Bob Pierce. That encounter years ago with an orphan child rocked his own complacency and gave birth to a vision, a World Vision. It's this idea that God's Kingdom Enterprise could and would move forward not through the mighty, not through the gifted, not through the moneyed, but through the weakest and smallest among us. Bob Pierce had a vision of children leading us forward in the Kingdom of God. He believed that championing children was the BIG thing God was doing.

For all his imperfections, Bob Pierce was truly a man after God's own heart. He had eyes to see and a heart to live in the paradox of the Kingdom of God. Great initiatives and world-changing events happen every day, but none of them start out that way. These opportunities are all around us, but we must have eyes to see. We must see life, and we must see others through Jesus' eyes.

When we look at the work God is doing in the world, the beginning point always looks remarkably the same. It's concealed behind distressing disguises, desperate needs, and vulnerable children. Every great work starts out as a simple and small opportunity to love.

I had my priorities all backwards for way too many years. At countless church conferences, I was treated with a vision of the world's greatest leaders, the church's most profound communicators, and the most inspiring works being done. I'm not writing to disparage that but to say within me a connection was not being made with the humble beginnings of every great work of God.

I owe my life to a young man who likely doesn't even remember my name. I was just one visitor among many who came to see the work he was doing. But a kid in a Soweto slum, on the backside of nowhere, is the epitome of how majestic and breathtaking the work of God actually is. Experiences like mine are meant to surprise us and to shock us back to the reality that the bigness of the work of God is contained in even the smallest heart that loves.

It was just a little boy who gave a sack lunch to feed a multitude. It was just a widow that deposited a couple of pennies in an offering box

22222

that inspired the world's greatest philanthropists. It was just a prostitute with a bottle of perfume who gave us the walking, breathing definition of extravagant love. It was a thief, dying for his crimes, guilty as charged, that taught us it's never too late to find forgiveness. The Kingdom of God is always breaking forth through the most unknown people in the most unspectacular ways.

The following poem is well known, written years ago by a man named Forest Witcraft. It is something I always thought was true, and at one level it is, but it's only a partial truth.

> "100 years from now it will not matter:
> What kind of car I drove.
> What kind of house I lived in.
> How much money I had in my account.
> Nor what my clothes looked like.
> But the world may be a little better.
> Because I was important in the life of a child." [3]

Like I said, at one level, these words are definitely true, but given the paradoxical nature of the Kingdom of God, given what Bob Pierce saw with spiritual eyes, there is something else even more profoundly true. It is vitally important to make a difference in the world's most vulnerable population, but that fact is only half of the equation.

You see, if I were writing this poem about the value of what my sponsor kids have brought to my life and if I were trying to describe what they have done for me and how the Kingdom of God actually works, I would be compelled to write instead;

> 100 years from now it will not matter:
> That my village was numbered among the poorest
> And my home made of mud and thatch.
> It will not matter that I never had a bank account
> Nor that my clothes were tattered and torn
> But the world may be a better place.
> Because I was important in the life of a pastor.

When I needed saving and was at the end of my rope and sick of playing church, I discovered the greatest truth of all: God hides his best treasures among the poor.

My plight reminds me of what Jean Vanier said to Henri Nouwen while Nouwen was teaching in the Ivy League. He told Nouwen that he was wasting his life there, and instead he should, "Go and live among the poor in spirit, and they will heal you." [4] His words are so true. He states what we've been missing and why we were so desperately wrong.

Cutting ourselves off from them has cut us off from a major conduit of God's healing love to us. What I've discovered is all the loving and giving I do pales in comparison with what returns to me. God has a special place in His heart for vulnerable people, and in the end, what He wants to know is not "What did you believe?" but "How did you love?"

An amazing little book was written over a hundred years ago by a guy named Henry Drummond called *The Greatest Thing in the World*. It's a commentary on 1 Corinthians 13. As Drummond wraps up his book, he makes this simple, yet totally profound statement (The passage he is writing about is Matthew 25 – I was hungry, did you feed me?)

> *"Sins of commission in that awful indictment are not even referred to. By what we have not done, by sins of omission, we are judged. It could not be otherwise. For the withholding of love is the negation of the spirit of Christ, the proof that we never knew Him, that for us He lived in vain. It means that He suggested nothing in all our thoughts, that He inspired nothing in all our lives, that we were not once near enough to Him to be seized with the spell of His compassion for the world. It means that:*
>
> *'I lived for myself,*
> *I thought for myself,*
> *For myself, and none beside—*
> *Just as if Jesus had never lived,*
> *As if He had never died.'"* [5]

(In the end, what God is looking for is a life radically changed toward the vulnerable people of this world. If we love Jesus, if we follow in His footsteps, and if His presence has accomplished anything in our life, first and foremost our hearts should be broken for the hungry, the thirsty, and the needy.)

"Let my heart be broken by the things that break the heart of God."
—DR. BOB PIERCE

"Oh, Lord, make it so."
—PASTOR KEITH STEWART

ENDNOTES

CHAPTER 1

1. Shane Claiborne, *The Irresistible Revolution: Living as an Ordinary Radical*, (Grand Rapids: Zondervan, 2006) 113.
2. Brian Peterson, Not Much to Celebrate in New Barna AIDS Survey, (http://www.worldvision.org/worldvision/pr.nsf/stable/new_barna) November 2002.
3. Henri J.M. Nouwen, *Bread for the Journey: A Daybook of Wisdom and Faith* (San Francisco: Harper Collins, 1996), entry for October 27th: "Forgiving the Church"
4. Ibid
5. Ibid
6. M. Scott Peck, *People of the Lie: The Hope for Healing Human Evil,* (New York: Touchstone, 1983)
7. Thomas Carlyle, *Lecture II, The Hero as a Prophet, Mahomet: Islam,* May 8, 1840.

CHAPTER 2

1. Access to Safe Water for the Base of the Pyramid, (http://www.hystra.com/opensource/Safe_Water_for_the_BoP.html) September 2011.
2. Ibid
3. World Health Organization, Fact sheet No.178, (http://www.who.int/mediacentre/factsheets/fs178/en/) September 2012.
4. Francis S. Collins, *Belief: Readings on the Reason for Faith* (New York, Harper Collins Publishers, 2010) 260.
5. Martin Luther King Jr., Strength to Love, 1963.

CHAPTER 3

1. R. Kent Hughes, *The Sermon on the Mount: The Message of the Kingdom, Volume 40,* (Wheaton: Crossway, 2001) 19.

Chapter 4

1. Eugene Peterson, *Working the Angles,* (Grand Rapids: Wm. B. Eerdmans Publishing Co., 1987) 1–2.
2. Marilee Dunker Pierce, *The Search for White Jade*, World Vision Chapel Service, Nov 10, 2010

Chapter 5

1. Poke London, (http://www.globalrichlist.com/).
2. Rich Stearns and Lamar Vest, *Christians losing their way,* The Washington Post: On Faith, Guest Voices, (http://newsweek.washingtonpost.com/onfaith/guestvoices/2009/12/call_for_christians_to_help_poor.html) December 14, 2009.

Chapter 6

1. Michael M. Phillips, *In Swaziland, U.S. Preacher Sees His Dream Vanish,* Wall Street Journal: U.S. Edition, Monday, December 19, 2005
2. Andy Crouch, *Experiencing Life at the Margins: An African bishop tells North American Christians the most helpful gospel-thing they can do,* Christianity Today, 7/1/2006

Chapter 7

1. Ched Myers, *God Speed the Year of Jubilee!,* Sojourners online journal, May-June 1998
2. Ron Sider, *Evangelical Liberation Theology,* Street Level Consulting (website)
3. Warren Wiersbe, *Wiersbe Bible Commentary OT,* (Colorado Springs: David C. Cook, 2007) 243.
4. USA Today, *Transcript: Bono remarks at the National Prayer Breakfast,* (http://usatoday30.usatoday.com/news/washington/2006–02–02-bono-transcript_x.htm) 2/2/2006.

Chapter 8

1. Bruce Larson, *Mastering the New Testament, Luke,* (Word, 1983) 39–40.
2. E. Stanley Jones, *Christ's Alternative to Communism,* (New York: The Abingdon Press, 1935) 54.
3. William Barclay, *The Gospel of Luke,* (Louisville: Westminster John Knox Press, 1975) 10.

4. Martin Luther, Works of Martin Luther: The Magnificat, translated and explained 1520–1, (http://www.godrules.net/library/luther/NEW1luther_c5.htm).

5. Walter Pilgrim, *Good News to the Poor: Wealth and Poverty in Luke-Acts,* (Eugene: Wipf and Stock Publishers, 1981) 14.

6. Comedy Central, *The Colbert Report: Jesus is a Liberal Democrat,* December 16, 2010

Chapter 9

1. Philip Edgcumbe Hughes, *The Second Epistle to the Corinthians: The New International Commentary of the New Testament,* (Grand Rapids: William B. Eerdmans Publishing Co., 1962) 307.

2. Shane Claiborne, *The Irresistible Revolution: Living as an Ordinary Radical,* (Grand Rapids: Zondervan, 2006) 170.

Chapter 10

1. Howard H. Covitz, PhD, March 30, 2000, Shabbos and Proper Nouns

2. Rodney Brown, *The Sermon on the Amount (Matthew 6:19–24),* (http://parkviewcc.net/sermons-messages/popup/text/print/71) January 27, 2013.

3. Martin Luther, "*The Larger Catechism,*" in *The Book of Concord,* ed. Theodore G. Tappert (Philadephia: Fortress Press, 1959) 365.

Chapter 11

1. Rick Rusaw and Eric Swanson, *The Externally Focused Church,* (Loveland: Group Publishing, 2004) 68.

2. Kenneth Bailey, *Jesus Through Middle Eastern Eyes,* (Downers Grove: InterVarsity Press, 2008) 303.

3. Klyne Snodgrass, *Stories with Intent: A Comprehensive Guide to the Parables of Jesus,* (Grand Rapids: Wm. B. Eerdmans Publishing Co., 2008) 399.

4. Eugene Peterson, *Tell It Slant: A Conversation on the Language of Jesus in His Stories and Prayers,* (Grand Rapids: Wm. B. Eerdmans Publishing Co., 2008) 62.

5. Arthur A. Just, *Luke,* (Downers Grove: InterVarsity Press, 2003) 208.

CHAPTER 12

1. Dan Graves, C. T. Studd Gave Huge Inheritance Away, (http://www.christianity.com/church/church-history/timeline/1801–1900/c-t-studd-gave-huge-inheritance-away-11630616.html) May, 2007.

2. A.W. Tozer, *The Pursuit of God*, (Harrisburg: Christian Publications, Inc. 1948) 18.

3. Scouting Around, *Within My Power - The Power of One Man*, (http://scoutingaround.com/boy-scouts/43-leadership/74-within-my-power-the-power-of-one-man.html) 2008.

4. Henri J.M. Nouwen, *In the Name of Jesus: Reflections on Christian Leadership*, (New York: The Crossroad Publishing Company, 1989) 11.

5. Henry Drummond, *The Greatest Thing in the World*, (Grand Rapids: Revell, 2012) 53–54.